20th CENTURY KETTERING

By the same author:

Kettering Revisited: Pictures from the Past (1993)
The Kettering Album: More Pictures from the Past (1997)

20th CENTURY KETTERING

A Book for the Millennium

Tony Smith

W. D. WHARTON
WELLINGBOROUGH

This book is dedicated to Mr Tony Ireson, the foremost exponent of Kettering's history and heritage in the twentieth century, without whose inspiration and encouragement the author's own trilogy of publications would not have appeared.

First published in 1999 by
W. D. Wharton
37 Sheep Street
Wellingborough
Northamptonshire NN8 1BX

ISBN 1-899597-08-5

Designed and typeset by John Hardaker
Wollaston, Northants
Printed and bound in Great Britain by
Butler & Tanner Ltd
Frome, Somerset

END-PAPER CAPTIONS

Front left: The old Kettering Grammar School building in Gold Street, circa 1963. (*Kettering Leader*)

Front right: Kettering Parish Church during the bitter winter of 1947. (*Tony Smith*)

Rear left: Spencer Percival's picture of the new Kettering Grammar School and Kettering High School building in Bowling Green Road in 1913. It is now the borough council offices. (*Tony Smith*)

Rear right: Pupils pictured outside Stamford Road School in the 1920s. (*Tony Smith*)

High Street, 1940s.

Contents

Acknowledgements

The photographs in this book come from the author's own collection or were taken by the author, except where duly credited. Words cannot express my gratitude to Leo Corvesor for allowing me to reproduce the wonderful colour transparencies taken by his late father, Frank Corvesor, and for agreeing to write the foreword.

I am indebted to the following people for the kind loan of photographs: Francis Watts, Judy Eden, Margaret Skelham, Graham Arber, John Barton, William Caswell, Queen Eleanor Ltd, Mary Green, Roger Warwick, Bob York, Kathleen Wells, Ted Sismore, Nathia Gray, Bill Lewin, Sid Green, Ken Fairey, Leslie Breed and Britannia Pink and Jones. Those pictures originally taken by the *Evening Telegraph* are also acknowledged with many thanks.

Other people who have helped me with research are: Malcolm Robinson and his staff at Kettering Reference Library, Catherine Nisbet at the Manor House Museum, Liz McBride at the *Evening Telegraph*, Northamptonshire Record Office, Nathia Gray, Bobby Civil, Jo Pearce, Roger West, Richard Seddon, Pete and Margaret Bridgman, Mel Hopkins, Paul Sharpling and Reg and Alan Carvell.

Special thanks must also go to publisher Robert Wharton for his continued support, the loan of photographs and postcards from his own collection, and for including the use of colour in this publication.

Bibliography

Kettering Leader (*and Guardian*) and Northamptonshire *Evening Telegraph*
Old Kettering and its Defenders (1984) by Tony Ireson
Old Kettering – A View from the 1930s, Volumes 1-5 (1988-1998) by Tony Ireson
Kettering: Temp George V (1912)
The Diamond Jubilee History of the Kettering Industrial Co-operative Society (1926)
Torchbearers in History: Half a Century of Co-operative Industrial Fellowship (1943)
An Industrial Republic 1888-1909 by W. Henry Brown
Memories of Midland Politics by Francis Channing (1918)
Growth and Goodwill: The New Way, by the Kettering Clothing Manufacturing Co-operative Society (1928)
The School in the Horsemarket by John Lilley (1951)
My Father by W. H. F. Timpson (1936)
Wallis and Linnell Ltd: A Hundred Years of Progress (1956)
75th Anniversary of United Counties by Roger Warwick (1988)
Kelly's Directory of Northamptonshire (various)
From Behind The Counter by Jane Evans (1996)

HVGH VABIS

THE PUBLIC LIBRARY.

From a sketch by

Hugh Wallis.

Foreword

After the success of Tony's first two volumes of photographs, *Kettering Revisited* and *The Kettering Album*, I found it hard to imagine that a third book in the series could match or better the high standards set previously. How wrong can you be! As soon as I saw this latest book, I knew that it was something very special.

20th Century Kettering not only covers the whole spectrum from Edwardian times to the present day, but it is larger than the previous two books and includes some exciting new features. Photographs and postcards, recreated using the latest imaging techniques, have given the book a new dimension.

The chapters recording scenes from local industries and shops are particularly fascinating and I am sure many readers will remember all the personalities and sporting heroes connected with the town in the section devoted to people. As an "old boy" of Kettering Grammar School, the photograph showing pupils and masters reminds me of happy days spent at the school in the 1950s, where I received an excellent education.

I am very pleased that Tony was able to use so many of my late father's colour slides in the centre section of the book. I'm sure they will complement all the other new photographs that Tony has presented to us.

My father loved his adopted town and was proud of it, but was also very saddened by the way so many beautiful buildings were demolished (some virtually overnight) in the crazy town centre redevelopment of the 1960s and 1970s. The old Grammar School in Gold Street, Beech House and the old Post Office buildings are

Bakehouse Hill

good examples. He was determined to preserve the memory of the changes in the town in his slide collection – little did he know that one day they would be shared with the rest of the town.

Some colour slide films had speeds of only 25ASA, which meant you had to have good light conditions and the sun shining on your subject from the right direction! It was a dedicated labour of love, which resulted in a unique set of pictures showing many parts of the town that have now, unfortunately, been lost forever.

He used to tell me about the idea Kettering Council had in the 1920s to widen Queen Street and Market Street, rebuild Dryland Street with new shops and create a town centre in the very heart of Kettering. Seventy years on and they are still discussing it! I often wonder what my father would have said about our new "merry-go-round" one-way road system.

When I first read this book, I thought how daunting a task it must have been to compile such a complex project. The years of diligent research, the writing and editing involved, not to mention amassing suitable photographs, was surely only a job for a true professional.

I'm sure you will agree Tony has produced a book which is superbly written, well-balanced and beautifully presented. I am convinced it will become a classic of its type. Hopefully it will be enjoyed by many, for browsing and reminiscing, and also by future generations who may want a glimpse of what Kettering was really like before the year 2000.

I warmly congratulate Tony on his magnificent book and wish it every success.

Leo F. Corvesor, Kettering, 1999

A Century of Change

Over the last millennium the world we live in and the way we live have changed immeasurably, but the relentless path of progress shifted up a gear or two during the twentieth century. From the pencil to the computer, from horse-drawn carriages to moon rockets, the passage from poverty to prosperity has been a tortuous process – a bumpy ride taking us through booms and recessions, dramas and disasters and two world wars.

Like elsewhere in Britain, Kettering has undergone a momentous metamorphosis over the past 100 years. This ancient market town, built on the back of a burgeoning boot and shoe industry, has developed into a modern, sprawling, expanding community, its population spiralling from 28,653 in 1901 to almost 50,000 (and still rising).

Along the way, almost inevitably, it has lost much of its character, not to mention some of its most attractive buildings, often needlessly. This book is an attempt to recapture Kettering's former glory in words and pictures (many in full colour), preserving the past for present and maybe future generations to enjoy. ·

Through these pages readers can return to those halcyon days when Kettering boasted five cinemas; more than 30 shoe factories; dozens of friendly family firms; a town centre teeming with shops providing personal service and home deliveries; a busy weekly market and cattle market; packed pubs panelled with wood (not plastic); a grammar school and a football team to be proud of.

By contrast, the story of the century is brought right up to date with photographs charting the phenomenal amount of new development, both outside and inside the town, since the controversial opening of the Newborough Centre in the 1970s and, more noticeably, since the new A14 link road opened in 1994.

The book also pays tribute to some of the well-known people who have helped shape or promote the town, served its residents, provided employment for entire families, or put it on the sporting and entertainment maps. This special chapter has been something of a personal odyssey, having met and got to know many of these local "celebrities" through my work on the *Evening Telegraph* (counting some as personal friends).

This is not intended to be a definitive roll of honour and deliberately avoids duplicating those featured in my previous two books (e.g. Charles Wicksteed and members of the Gotch family). I accept many others would be equally worthy of a mention, but hope readers will appreciate the space limitations in trying to cover so many important facets of the town in such a publication.

The alarming speed of change in Kettering since I began preparing this book has played havoc with my writing. All the captions (I trust) are correct at the time of "going to press", yet even as I write there are plans pending to knock down the old Drill Hall, the former Savoy cinema and the *ET*'s ancestral home in Dryland Street. Two metal monstrosities resembling alien spacecraft have also materialised at Tanners Gate behind dear old Beech Cottage; building work is progressing on yet another "much-needed" giant supermarket (off Lower Street); and there are welcome proposals to revive the Central Hall as a major music venue.

No doubt there will be many other surprises in store for Kettering and its people in the coming century. I have no crystal ball, but in an increasingly uncertain future, there are only two cast-iron guarantees during the next 100 years: (1) every few seasons the Poppies will spoil their chances of promotion to the Football League, despite topping the table for weeks on end, and (2) every 20 years a new road system will be introduced in the town, creating far more problems than it solves.

Let's hope the good burghers who decide the town's destiny in the next 100 years will try harder to get things right.

Tony Smith, Summer, 1999

1. Early Years

Kettering began the twentieth century with a population of around 28,500 and most of those residents turned out for festivities to mark the coronation of King Edward VII and Queen Alexandra on Saturday, 9 August 1902. Arrangements were decided by a 40-strong committee led by local businessman Alfred Webb, and the £500 cost was met by public subscription. After morning services at Kettering Parish Church and Fuller Chapel, a huge procession around the town was led by the Northants Yeomanry, the Chief Constable (Supt. Andrews) on horseback and Kettering Rifle Band. Prizes were awarded for best entries judged at the Cattle Market and Manor House Field. In the afternoon there was a parade by 7,000 schoolchildren and each was presented with a commemorative medal, followed by tea in Headlands. Sports and entertainment were then held in Headlands playing fields, and the day ended with a spectacular fireworks display.
Pictured is the crowded High Street after the morning procession had passed. (*Tony Smith*)

Kettering Library

A horse drinks from the trough of the Dryland Memorial outside Kettering Library, officially opened on 7 May 1904. The £8,000 building was presented to the town by philanthropist Andrew Carnegie, who also attended the opening ceremony. Previously the town had a temporary library of 1,650 volumes in the Corn Exchange (1896) and the Victoria Hall Mission premises in Silver Street (1901). The impressive Sheep Street building was designed by Messrs Goddard and Co, winners of an open competition of more than 70 entries assessed by architect J. A. Gotch. The Dryland Memorial, erected in 1907 as a tribute to Dr John Winter Dryland, lost its two troughs in 1947 following the demise of horse transport. Replacements costing £4,000 were unveiled in 1995 after a campaign by Kettering Civic Society. (*Tony Smith*)

The interior view of the library as seen on entering the original revolving doors. Extra storage space and a staff room were provided in 1936 and a separate children's section was established in 1949. The reading room was reduced to accommodate a new gramophone-record library in 1967 and by the 1970s book issues had risen to 530,000 per year, compared to 64,000 when the library opened. The building underwent a major £250,000 face-lift in 1986, during which the interior was repaired and remodelled to increase usable space by almost a third. Changes included a new computerised book-issue system and disabled access via the new side entrance. (*Tony Smith*)

A typical Temperance procession passes Smith & Sons (now Lewins) in High Street in the early part of the century. The Temperance movement has existed in the town for more than 160 years and its present premises in Gold Street were bought in 1864. In the Victorian and Edwardian eras, its Band of Hope would appear in local parades, rallies and open-air meetings as its God-fearing members denounced the demon drink as the greatest social evil. Early campaigners included Charles Pollard, engineer Owen Robinson and draper Frederic Wallis. Today Kettering Temperance Society has 75 members who hold regular meetings and social events to raise money.
In recent years its role has expanded to promoting abstinence from any drugs or addictions and its two full-time officers liaise with police, the youth service and the Council on Addiction, giving talks to local schools and church groups. (*Tony Smith*)

The Liberal Club

Kettering's handsome Liberal Club in Dalkeith Place was erected in 1889 as the headquarters of local Liberals following the creation, four years earlier, of the new East Northants constituency and consequent widening of the electorate. Costing £3,400, the Jacobean-style building was designed by Gotch and Saunders and featured a comfortable lounge, billiard room, offices and assembly hall. From its imposing balcony, many mass meetings were addressed and election results declared. In more recent years it became a branch of the Trustee Savings Bank, Choi's Cantonese restaurant and currently Xtra, a public house owned by the Mansfield Brewery. It remains arguably the town's most striking building. (*Tony Smith*)

The Liberal Club won first prize for the best decorated building on Coronation Day in 1902. Bedecked with bunting, plants and mottos, it also boasted hundreds of coloured electric lamps which lit up at night. Second prize went to the Workhouse in London Road (now St Mary's Hospital). The award for best decorated business premises went to Newland Street florist and seedsman Mr W. Toseland, with Webb Bros, the High Street tailors, runners-up. (*Tony Smith*)

Spencer Percival's busy balcony scene shows celebrations at the Liberal Club following the declaration of the 1906 election results, when every constituency in the county returned a Liberal member. In East Northants it was a sixth triumph for Lord Francis Aliston Channing (*inset*), after previous victories in 1885, 1886, 1892, 1895 and 1900. His majority was increased to 3,603, defeating rival Tory candidate Sir Arthur de Capell Brooke of Oakley Hall. Lord Channing is seen here addressing the crowds, with his daughter (in white furs) by his side. Also on the balcony, from left, are Mr F. W. Roughton, Mr W. F. Dorr, William Meadows (holding hat), Frank Mobbs (chairman of Kettering Urban Council), Thomas Wallis, Frank Toseland (Channing's agent), the Rev W. L. Lee, Mrs Wicksteed with daughter Hilda, James Heygate and John Turner Stockburn. Lord Channing was in bed with flu when he won his final election in January 1910 and resigned through ill health that December. He died in February 1926, aged 84, and as a mark of respect a flag was flown at half mast at the club. (*Tony Smith*)

Kettering Police Station

Kettering's old police station in London Road was an imposing Victorian building, erected in 1851. It was modified and enlarged in 1909, with new buildings designed by county surveyor Mr C. S. Morris and erected by local contractor Mr O. P. Drever. A large crowd saw Col S. G. Stopford Sackville, chairman of the county council, perform the official opening ceremony on Wednesday, 11 August 1909, attended by Supt. Hooper, Insp. Tebbey, 30 constables and four sergeants, the latter wearing new white summer hats. In those days, experts considered this building, used for the first time for the weekly Petty Sessions (now Magistrates Court), to be one of the best of its kind in the country. (*Tony Smith*)

The Swan Inn

A splended photograph of two horse-drawn brakes, loaded all ready for a day's outing, outside the Swan Inn in Montagu Street circa 1912. The confectionery shop on the left, with chocolate adverts on the windows, has long gone and the area is now used as the pub's car park. (*Tony Smith*)

Veteran Salvation Army founder General William Booth (*also inset*) salutes the Kettering crowds during his visit on Thursday, 18 July 1907, part of his fourth motor preaching tour, taking in an incredible 72 towns in one month. He arrived in Kettering at 2.40pm, greeted by huge crowds which thronged London Road from Broadway to Dalkeith Place, Silver Street and Gold Street. Throughout the journey, the General, then aged 78, stood waving, Papal-style, wearing a field marshal's uniform. At Victoria Hall in Gold Street he was met by urban council chairman Thomas Adams and spontaneous applause erupted as he entered the building to music played by the Salvation Army Band. The *Kettering Leader* reported: "With his dominant nose and patriarchal beard he looked a chief, every inch of him. He is a magnificent dogmatist with a magnetic self-confidence."
After a rousing address, the General had tea with Mr J. T. Stockburn at the Mission House in Lower Street before setting off for Peterborough, via Thrapston and Oundle, at 6pm. Forty years earlier, General Booth had spoken at the town's Toller Church, staying the night at the Royal Hotel. (*Tony Smith*)

Rockingham Road was a blaze of colour as all the tradesmen between Regent Street and King Street celebrated the coronation of King George V and Queen Mary on Thursday, 22 June 1911. The town raised £600 for festivities (a lavish £60 for decorations alone!) and prizes were awarded for the prettiest houses, shops and factories in each street on the route of the official procession. Arches proclaiming "Long Live The King" were erected in the town centre and a huge canopy on the Market Place was held up by red, white and blue poles.
The Liberal Club had a grand floral display on its balcony and the Workhouse boasted large portraits of the Royal couple above its entrance. More than 7,000 coronation mugs were given to children attending special teas in Headlands and Broadway, and 520 OAPs enjoyed tea at the Victoria Hall. Church bells rang from 6am to 7am and there were special services before the parade (so big it took 26 minutes to pass) set off from the Manor House Field at 11am. Because of rain in the afternoon, a planned programme of sports, entertainment and fireworks in Headlands playing fields was postponed until the next day. (*Tony Smith*)

World War I

During World War I, Kettering's VAD (Voluntary Aid Detachment) Hospital in London Road cared for injured men, not only from Kettering but also from Welsh, Scottish, Irish, Canadian, Australian and New Zealand regiments. Under honorary surgeon Dr Lee, patients would often be treated to a day's entertainment, courtesy of Charles Wicksteed several years before his park officially opened. This picture, taken on 21 May 1915, shows Lady Supt. Farmer, Supt. Nurse Bloxham and other VAD staff members with the first 20 wounded soldiers received at the sanatorium. The hospital had been prepared for months by Kettering ambulance workers under the command of Lady Supt. Farmer from the St John Ambulance Brigade. Everything was ready, with pyjamas, bed jackets and bed socks neatly laid out on beds. The unit was staffed by six nursing sisters and two quartermasters, with three privates as orderlies, and Kettering people responded to an appeal for furniture, garden chairs, piano and gramophone, and they donated groceries and magazines. The second photograph shows four invalids on an excursion to Kettering Market Place. (*Tony Smith* and, right, *Robert Wharton*)

World War I

Towards the end of World War I, Kettering was presented with a tank, the Army's way of saying "thank you" to its citizens for helping to raise about £2 million in war savings. It weighed 28 tons and was a "female" (supposedly more vicious than the "male"!).
After leaving Kettering railway station, the vehicle rumbled through the town centre, with crowds lining the streets to watch its progress. Here it is pictured passing the former Wesleyan Chapel (now the Salvation Army Citadel) at the Rockingham Road junction with Regent Street. (*Robert Wharton*)

The tank is pictured at its final destination of Rockingham Road Pleasure Park, where a civic ceremony marked the occasion. Here it was parked on concrete strips outside the old bandstand, where it remained for several years as a reminder of what the townspeople had done. Two field guns which also stood with the tank were later moved to Legion Crescent. The huts in the background of the photograph were used as billets. (*Robert Wharton*)

Neighbours watch as two men cook with sawdust instead of coal in the back yard of a house in St Andrew's Street, Kettering. The photo was taken in June 1921 during the national fuel shortage caused by the miners' pay dispute. The miners had been locked out by pit owners on 1 April, and by May coal supplies had been practically exhausted. Big queues for coke could be seen throughout the day outside Kettering gasworks until the gas company, acting under orders of the Board of Trade, issued notices that all coke at the works was to be reserved for butchers, bakers, hospitals and other essential cases such as the aged and infirm. Gas supplies were rationed, only available from 6am to 1pm and 8pm to 10pm, upsetting families who found this inconvenient. All street lighting was reduced by 50 per cent, and at Kettering Station only two gas lamps were lit, leaving the booking office and platforms in darkness. To prevent accidents, oil lamps were hung in the subway. (*Tony Smith*)

Kettering Fire Station

For the first quarter of the century Kettering Fire Station was a rickety old building in Market Street. Until the motor era arrived, the town's two steam fire engines were pulled by horses brought from the Royal Hotel stables. A new station, costing £1,530, was opened lower down Market Street on Thursday, 22 October 1926 by urban council chairman George Chester, who described the previous building as a "positive eyesore". The replacement was a credit to the town, complete with bathroom, recreation room, workshop and drill tower (in later years the building was used as the town's ambulance station). There was constant pressure for a full-time brigade, but the town's finances did not run to anything more than a volunteer service. (*Robert Wharton*)

Captured for posterity in the late 1920s is Kettering's solid-tyred Leyland fire engine with its two-wheeled escape ladder. The brigade also had a Dennis motor engine, bought in 1917 and housed at Robinson's garage in Montagu Street (for £52 rent per year) because the old station was not big enough. This picture was taken in Gas Street (now Meadow Road), with a dutiful policeman keeping an eye on proceedings. On the left we can just see Halford's cycle shop. Kettering firemen used to hold annual competitions in the Manor House Field, followed by tea at the Cross Keys Tavern in Dalkeith Place. (*Tony Smith*)

Saturday, 11 September 1926 was a red-letter day for local Baptists when the stone-laying ceremony for the new Rockingham Road School Chapel took place. The building, part of the Fuller Mission in Oakley Street, cost £8,000 and a number of stones were laid by Oakley Street organisations, including the Sunday School, both the Young Men's and Young Women's Bible classes and the Mission Band. Former Fuller pastor, the Revd Thomas Phillips is seen giving his address to the large gathering of ministers, deacons, elders, Sunday School teachers and other church members. After the ceremony there was a tea in the Rockingham Road council schools, followed by an evening meeting chaired by the Reverend Ewan Williams. The building underwent major renovations, including the replacement of the roof and front entrance, in 1996. The £150,000 cost was raised by the 130-strong congregation. (*Tony Smith*)

An evocative picture of the (little-changed) frontage to Kettering General Hospital facing Rothwell Road. 1997 marked the centenary of KGH, built and funded by local people until the introduction of the National Health Service in 1948. The original building, on land donated by the Duke of Buccleuch, was designed by Gotch and Saunders and built by Alfred Barlow. At first there were two adult wards of ten beds (Buccleuch and Spencer), with room for two children's cots in each ward, plus a private ward with just two beds. Other facilities included a fully-equipped operating room, drug store, kitchen, dining room, matron's office and sleeping accommodation for five nurses. Each ward was heated by two stoves, lit by gas burners, and boasted bay windows overlooking the grounds, where a vegetable garden and orchard produced fresh food for patients. The first X-ray department opened in 1905, followed by a separate eye department in 1908 and a children's ward in 1922 in an area originally earmarked for discharged soldiers in 1918. By the 1920s the hospital's workload had risen sevenfold since its opening, treating almost 2,000 people a year – more than half as in-patients. (*Tony Smith*)

Nurses at Kettering General Hospital line up to welcome the Duke of Buccleuch for the official opening of the new nurses' home on the afternoon of Saturday, 1 May 1926 – ironically the first day of the General Strike. The Duke, using architect J. A. Gotch's silver key, ceremonially unlocked the door of the £9,000 building, erected on more land he had generously donated. It was named Warren Hill House and provided 31 rooms for nurses and sisters (at that time there was a complement of 22 nurses, one of them private). A platform in front of the main entrance was packed with VIPs, chaired by Frank Berrill, hospital president and treasurer of the Board of Management. (*Tony Smith*)

In 1996 the women's section of the Kettering branch of the Royal British Legion celebrated its 70th anniversary with a birthday tea and social evening at the Corn Market Hall. Early records reveal that the first chairman and secretary were Mrs Ethel Everitt and Mrs Timpson respectively, and early meetings were held at the USF Club in Meeting Lane. This picture shows the group's first standard bearer, Mrs Atwell, leading a parade outside Bradshaw Stores (now Victoria Wine) in Dalkeith Place in 1929. The original standard cost £4. 4s. 6d. (£4.22) and the badge was bought for two shillings (10p). The ladies gave coal and groceries to the needy at Christmas and milk and nourishment to sick children. During the 1930s they backed a campaign to appoint Kettering's first policewoman. In its heyday the women's section boasted 400 members, but in recent years numbers have dropped to 100, mostly aged 60 to 80. They still meet twice a month. (*Kathleen Wells*)

This early postcard by Spencer Percival is a rare and interesting view taken from the George Street corner of the George Hotel looking back along Sheep Street to the Market Place, before road widening. On the left is the Cherry Tree, one of Kettering's oldest inns (believed to date back to the early seventeenth century) and on the opposite side of the road is the former Albion Temperance Hotel at the foot of old Market Hill, demolished in 1936. For many years the hotel was kept by Mr W. Palmer, a member of a well-known Kettering family – one of his brothers founded Palmer's Music Stores in Dalkeith Place, another owned a tailoring business, and all were prominent in the musical life of the town. (*Tony Smith*)

With early motor cars way beyond the means of the ordinary working man, the first mode of transport enjoyed by many was the humble motor cycle (and if you wanted to take the wife and/or children for a ride, you just added a sidecar). Gear boxes and kick-starters were unknown in the early part of the century and it wasn't until World War I that the motorbike came of age. Pictured here are committee members of Kettering and District Motor Cycling Club astride their machines outside Kettering Library in 1914. (*Tony Smith*)

Those of you who bought my first book *Kettering Revisited* may remember the superb shot of despatch riders pictured on their motor cycles at the rear of the police station in the 1920s. This picture, taken from the same spot, shows early traffic officers with their pre-Panda open-top motors. The first cars used by county police in the 1930s were BSA three-wheelers. (*Tony Smith*)

Mother and Baby Week

A fascinating photo of one of the displays at the Child Welfare Exhibition in the Corn Market Hall as part of Kettering Mother and Baby Week in May 1930. Mums and tots also had tea in the hall after the traditional pram parade around the town centre on the opening Saturday. That evening there was a fête in the grounds of Chesham House in Lower Street, featuring country dancers from the School Lane Centre dancing class, trained by Miss J. Tomalin. The prizewinning pram belonged to Mrs West of Carlton Street and champion babies – both breast-fed and open-air babies – were Mary Winter of Edgar Road (under 12 months) and Jessie Wildman of Wellington Street (one to two years). The exhibition was opened by Mrs J. R. Clynes, wife of the Home Secretary and one of many Cabinet Ministers' spouses invited as special guests. Also reproduced here is an illustrated postcard to advertise the event. (*Tony Smith*)

I must admit, this is one of my favourite postcards of Kettering, dating from the late 1930s. What makes it so intriguing is the detail, from the road sign to Stamford to the different forms of transport (car, bus, bike and barrow!). Taken from the top of Gold Street and looking along Newland Street, businesses on the right-hand side include Woodcocks the drapers, the Mikado Café, the Co-op Arcade (and clock), KICS Central Stores and the Fleur de Lys pub. But best of all is the bobby on point duty at the crossroads, standing on top of a crate in front of the bollards to ensure he can be seen by road users from all directions. (*Tony Smith*)

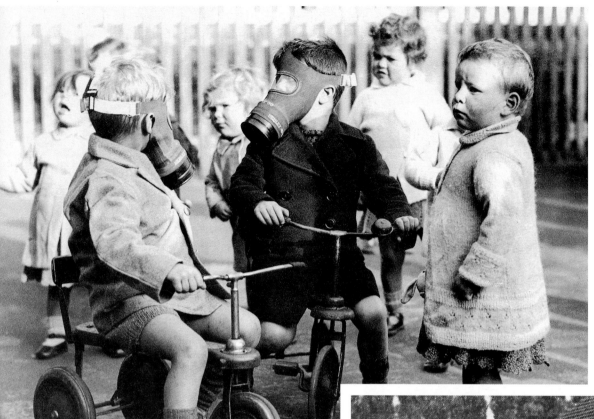

World War II

As war clouds gathered over Europe in 1939, plans were made to evacuate children from London and other cities to areas less prone to air attacks. These mites with their gas masks were among the first 13,000 to arrive in special trains at Kettering station during the first weekend in September. The first train carried 800 children from Hackney, Kentish Town, Camden and Islington. They were met by 15 reception officers who took them to local schools used as distribution centres. There they were given food and drink before being taken door-knocking to find their new families. It was difficult to find homes for some children because they were so dirty and in rags. Those who couldn't be put up in Kettering were bussed to 28 villages in the borough. The evacuees shared schools with the locals on a shift system and some enjoyed Kettering so much that they stayed with their adoptive families or returned later to live in the area. (*Tony Smith*)

Ramparts of sandbags are stacked outside the portico of St Luke's Ward at Kettering General Hospital during World War II. To cope with the expected influx of war-wounded, auxiliary nurses were specially trained at Kettering General, and the Smallpox Hospital in Rockingham Road was put on standby in case of infectious disease among evacuees from London slums. Some 60 per cent of all in-patients at KGH were sent home within hours of war being declared and a number of beds were reserved for emergency cases only. Wounded soldiers were entitled to an extra hot meal – a cooked supper – which made fellow patients jealous. All building work at the hospital was suspended during the war years. (*Tony Smith*)

As with other towns, Kettering had its own "Dad's Army" during World War II. Within ten minutes of Mr Eden's radio appeal for volunteers on 14 May 1940, hundreds of men besieged Kettering's police station, and the local battalion was commanded by the town's rector, the Reverend G. Holborrow. The Home Guard, as it became known, was split into various platoons, each with their own Captain Mainwaring, taking part in regular drills and exercises at evenings and weekends. On this page is "H" Company, 24th Platoon, 4th Battalion, photographed in 1942 in front of Dr Roughton's old house next to the United Counties garage at the top of Northampton Road. The men, who worked at the bus depot, are (left to right) – back row: Privates Torlot, Smith, Phillips, Toseland, Walker. Third row: Privates Edwards, Swain, Gardiner, Asher, Hill, Drew, Symonds, Carrington, Bradley, Gore, Walklate, Mabbutt, Park, Smart. Second row: Private Morgan, Sgts Barker and Lowe, Lts Andrews and Vicars, Sgt Ball, Cpls Bulley and Kerr. Front row: Privates Hammond, Chapman, Arnold, Bye, Sirrell, Adams. (*Roger Warwick*)

Kettering Baths played a major role in the life of the town before being replaced by the present pool complex in London Road in January 1984. When the indoor pool (top) first opened in March 1915, separate timetables were arranged each day for ladies and gentlemen, who paid charges of 2d to 4d. Between the wars, in addition to staging local and regional swimming galas and water polo matches, a floor was erected over the pool for dances, meetings, indoor sports events such as boxing, grand dinners and other social events (see two pictures below). It was the practice to empty the pool at 4pm on Saturday for cleaning purposes and water was discharged into a brook which ran under the Avondale estate. Saturday night bands included Len Hustler, Harry Richards, the Saxoleans, the Dixie Coons, Ritz Players, Tommy Ashby and Charlie Walker. The legendary violinist Yehudi Menuhin even performed there. (*Margaret Skelham*)

It seems hard to imagine that Kettering once had this wonderful "lido" – the open-air swimming pool with its diving platform, water chute and sun-bathing terrace. The town first had an outdoor pool in the early 1800s, funded by local shoemakers. But, at the turn of this century, this was taken over by the urban council, which embarked on an ambitious conversion plan. At a cost of £6,400 the existing pool, measuring 240ft by 46ft, was divided in two to provide one outdoor and one covered, heated pool. Major improvements to the outdoor pool, costing £4,000, were carried out in 1935 and more than 700 people attended the re-opening ceremony by council chairman Cllr Mayes on 9 July. There was a new refreshment booth and offices, new locker system to protect patrons' clothes, showers and deck chairs, and an up-to-date filtration plant, making the water on a par with the town's drinking supply. At that time the facilities at Kettering were said to be second to none in the country.
(*Margaret Skelham*)

One chilling tradition was maintained during the 1930s by a hardy group of all-year-round bathers. Every Christmas morning, come rain, shine or even snow, these merry "madmen" insisted on their seasonal dip, even when, as on this occasion, a blanket of ice had formed on the surface on the outdoor pool! Also pictured (*inset*) is the familiar face of the late Mary Bonham, the formidable instructress who taught generations of Kettering people to swim. For 41 years, until retiring in 1977, Miss Bonham instructed children from 22 schools in the borough, helping them gain 1,250 water safety awards a year. In 1952 she coached the All England Boys' Swimming Champions and the East Midlands District Champions and in 1968 set up Kettering Life Saving Club. She died in February, 1989, aged 73, and part of the redeveloped pool site in Bath Lane is named Bonham Court in her honour. (*Margaret Skelham*)

2. Industry

The Kettering Clothing Manufacturing Co-operative Society began in 1893 with a dozen willing helpers and a small capital of £500, initially working from a wooden shed. Two years later a four-storey factory was erected in Dryden Street, close to the site of the old windmill, officially opened by the great trade unionist Thomas Burt. In 1901 a Burton Latimer branch was opened to make children's clothing and after various extensions to Dryden Street a new factory was built in 1913 on the corner of nearby Cobden Street and Field Street for the exclusive manufacture of ladies' clothing. In 1920 a Corby branch was added, specialising in youths' clothing, and by 1939 "Kaycee", as the firm became known, employed 1,639 people – 1,286 of them women. During World War II they made more than 500,000 military garments for the British and US Armies and the company was honoured with a visit by the King and Queen in March 1943. Being a co-operative, workers enjoyed a share in profits and social facilities included their own sports ground for football, hockey, tennis and cricket, plus tennis courts at Kettering and Corby. During the recession of the 1970s, Kaycee closed with the loss of 200 jobs. Pictured here are machinists in the Ladies' Costume Factory in Cobden Street circa 1925. Today the building is used by Seddon Packaging and Print. (*Tony Smith*)

1997 saw the centenary of Queen Eleanor, the successful clothing company, which began life as the town's Co-operative Corset Society. Generations of Kettering families have worked at its three-storey factory in Rutland Street. The firm was founded by former employees of the Stockburn corset factory in Northall Street and production began from small premises in Tanners Lane in November 1897.
The 12-strong workforce toiled round the clock to make samples to be sold to co-operative stores and within five years membership had swelled to 150, working from Rutland Street premises previously used by the Phipps brewery. Some of the men and women are pictured at work in the early part of the century. (*Queen Eleanor*)

Tea break in the Queen Eleanor machine room half a century ago. When fashions changed and corset sales declined, the firm turned in the 1950s to slips, nighties, housecoats and knickers, with record sales leading to sister factories opening in Corby, Thrapston and Ruskington in Lincolnshire. By the swinging sixties, Kettering underwear was being sold to women in Denmark, Norway, Sweden and Mauritius, but when the bottom (!) fell out of the lingerie market in the early 1980s, another change was needed for survival – hence the move to the corporate clothing and fashion overalls produced today by a 100-strong workforce. The firm is still run on traditional co-operative lines and remains one of only two manufacturing co-operatives left in Britain. (*Queen Eleanor*)

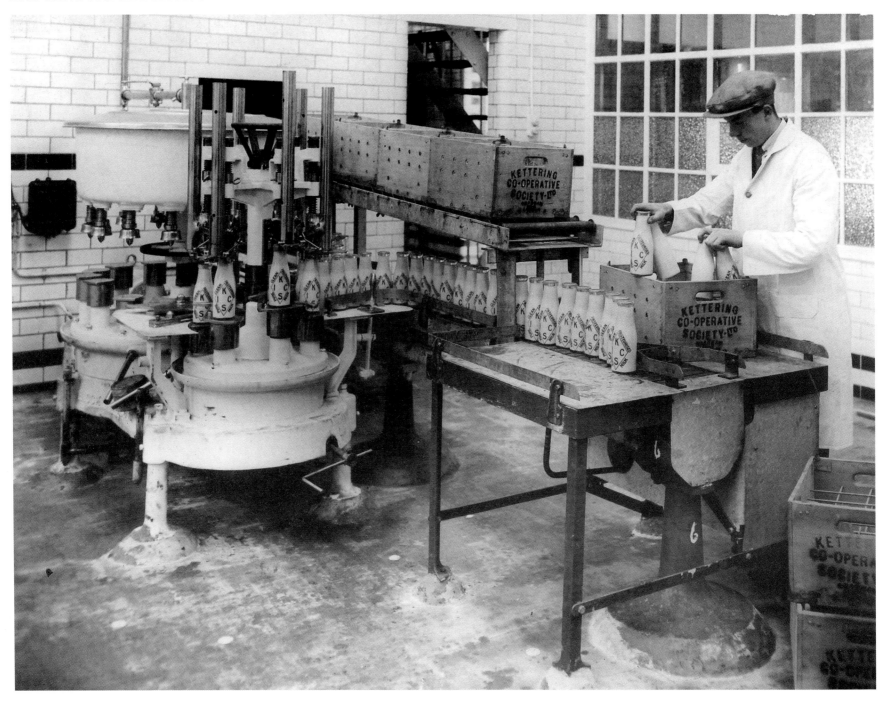

Everyone who can recall the first quarter of the century will remember the milkmen who delivered by horse-drawn float, filling their cans from a churn and measuring the milk into your jug at your front door – a process very much at the mercy of dust and germs. So it was a great step forward when the Kettering Industrial Co-operative Society opened its new model dairy in Neale Avenue in 1927 and began to deliver milk in sealed bottles, seen here being packed in wooden crates. To canvas for customers, the wily KICS began its new venture by delivering a free pint of milk to every house in the town. (*Tony Smith*)

A wonderful photograph of roundsmen lined up outside the old KICS dairy, ready for the off, shortly after the business was launched in the 1920s. The Co-op had expected the future Prime Minister Neville Chamberlain (then just a Cabinet member) to perform the official opening ceremony, but he was engaged elsewhere. Early milk "vans" were oblong, box-like affairs, riding on two large wooden wheels and two smaller ones with hard rubber tyres. The model dairy building, one of Kettering's landmarks, occupied a site bounded by Neale Avenue, Shakespeare Road and Blandford Avenue. After closing in the late 1970s, it was sold to developers who built two houses and seven bungalows there after the dairy was demolished in December 1982. (*Tony Smith*)

The Robinson Car

Kettering had its own mini motor industry in the early part of the century when an enterprising young engineer called Charles Robinson made a 12-horsepower four-cylinder car which was to go down in history. The 1907 two-seater, currently on display at the Manor House Museum, was the last of three vehicles designed and assembled by Robinson at his garage in Montagu Street. He built it for Dr J. P. Roughton at a cost of £235, the casting and much of the machining of parts being carried out at the Robinson family's shoe machinery factory in Victoria Street.

The car boasted a top speed of 47mph and an unusual cooling system using exhaust gases instead of water. There was also a purpose-built platform instead of a back seat, used as an emergency "operating table" when the doctor was away from his surgery or the hospital.

Subsequent owners over the years included car connoisseurs Graham Stock and Alan Bannell, the latter pictured at the wheel in 1982 when it was feared this unique part of Kettering's heritage would be sold to an American collector. A joint campaign to keep it in the town was waged by Kettering Civic Society and the Wicksteed Village Trust, which raised the asking price of £9,500 with the help of a £4,000 grant from the South Kensington Science Museum. The fate of the other two cars made by Robinson – both four-seater models – is unknown. (*Evening Telegraph*)

CHURCH WALK STEAM LAUNDRY, (J. H. Wilmot, proprietor.)

GOOD WORK

Moderate Charges

LAUNDRY,
DRY CLEANING,
DYE WORKS.

Note only address :—

CHURCH WALK.

Starched collars were the order of the day when this picture was taken inside Kettering Steam Laundry in the early 1920s. In 1919 the former dry cleaning and dye works, situated in Church Walk behind the police station, acquired a new boiler to produce steam for driving the plant and heating the presses. Weighing more than eight tons, it was transported from the railway station on a special low-built lorry pulled by five dray horses. The business merged with the Sleaford Group of laundries in 1965, but closed in March 1971 after 82 years of operation. It was sold outright to Sleaford because of the ill health of manager Bernard Wilmot, whose grandfather founded the firm in premises where he previously made old original whalebone corsets! KICS bought the laundry in 1973 and two years later it became a furniture showroom after various schemes were rejected, including a pub, night club, squash club and car showroom. (*Tony Smith*)

Skilled hand lasters at work at boot and shoe firm Allen and Caswell in the 1920s. The company, which now specialises in equestrian footwear, celebrated its centenary in 1997 as one of only two surviving shoe firms in Kettering (the other being Loake Bros in Wood Street). The business was founded by two friends, engineer Freddie Allen and Bertie Caswell, who previously worked for Rushden shoe giants Cave and Son. They began with a small factory in Albert Street, and after moves to Northall Street and Sackville Street they established their present premises in Cornwall Road in 1905. Using the latest machinery, the firm made such brand names as Campbells, Artisans and Clarence boots and shoes, and during World War I, it supplied boots for Russian and Italian forces, as well as our own troops (*William Caswell*)

Allen and Caswell

Women working in the closing room of Allen and Caswell around 1920. The firm pioneered "guarantee tags", took out the first patent for protective shoes in 1929 and was the first to incorporate the zip into footwear. In the 1920s, following the Russian Revolution, the Russians resorted to bartering for goods, adding cases of the Czar's own champagne to Mr Allen's and Mr Caswell's wine cellars! (*William Caswell*)

Life inside the clicking room of Allen and Caswell during the 1920s. To meet increasing demand, the firm bought the Drage Shoe Company in Bozeat in 1931 and when US forces took over its Kettering premises as a depot in World War II, production was switched to a factory in Connaught Street – then owned by Frank Wright and Company. During the 1950s the company began to specialise in sportswear, such as riding boots, football boots and boots for bowls, golf and skiing. It made cricket shoes for former Middlesex and England batsman Peter Parfitt in 1965 and motor cycle boots for pop star and actor Adam Faith in 1970. In 1989 the firm received the ultimate accolade when it earned the coveted Queen's Award for Export Achievement for its "Heritage" line of welted footwear. (*William Caswell*)

Factory days out were all the rage in Kettering in the 1950s. More than 500 employees, relatives and friends at clothing manufacturers Wallis and Linnell left the rain behind in 1956 for a sunnier day in Blackpool. The firm chartered a special train (above) of 15 dining cars so that breakfast could be served after the early start, leaving Kettering at 6am on Friday, 7 June. The next day a further 1,000 people left the town on three special trains to Blackpool, Southend and London – all employees of William Timpson Ltd of Kettering and the Avalon Boot Manufacturers of Rothwell.
(*Tony Smith*)

It was real men's work in the sweat and toil of Kettering Furnaces, which was a local landmark this century until 1959. Kettering Iron and Coal Company began operations off Rockingham Road in 1878, at first working district quarries by hand, wheeling the iron ore in barrows across narrow plank bridges. Later little narrow gauge trains puffed to and from the works, which began with two blast furnaces, each producing 250 tons of iron a week. A third was built by the turn of the century, to be replaced with a much larger furnace in 1908, capable of producing 1,000 tons a week. By the early 1930s the plant was virtually rebuilt to raise output at full production to 100,000 tons of iron per year. At their height the furnaces employed 600 men, with three generations of some families working for the company. Their glowing embers were extinguished in 1959, along with other works at Cranford, Irchester, Loddington, Cransley and Wellingborough, and the plant was demolished four years later. (*Tony Smith*)

Timpsons

For 50 glorious years the William Timpson shoe factory in Bath Road provided work for Kettering people. The imposing building, which began production in 1923, was considered an architectural marvel at the time. Unlike other local shoe factories built in pokey Victorian backstreets, it was one of the finest examples of early reinforced concrete construction, and large expanses of windows soon earned it the nickname of "the Crystal Palace". After it closed in 1972, the factory was bought by the British Shoe Corporation and it ended its days as part of the ill-fated Burlington International Group. It was truly the end of an era when the building was demolished in 1996 to make way for private housing. (*Tony Smith*)

William Timpson Ltd prided itself as an employer which really cared for its workforce. The use of so much glass in its construction, coupled with the latest type of cold cathode lighting, made the new factory a joy to work in. The building stood in pleasant gardens, complete with bowling green and tennis courts for the use of employees. There were also works outings and this picture taken in Bath Road shows a line of Leyland Lion buses hired for just such an occasion during the 1930s. (*Tony Smith*)

Women working in the closing room at Timpsons in January 1960. After the founder's death in 1929 (because of his illness he never set foot in his revolutionary factory), the company came under the control of his two sons, joined later by his grandsons and great grandsons, going from strength to strength. By 1939 it owned 195 shops, and the shoe repair business increased rapidly after the war. New methods of manufacture were introduced in the 1950s, with hundreds of thousands of men's fine grade welted shoes exported to the USA. When this picture was taken, there were more than 250 Timpson shoe shops, over 150 repair workshops and 4,500 employees. When Timpsons closed in 1972, many of the remaining 800 workers left the building with tears in their eyes. (*Kettering Leader*)

Frank Wright's Standard Works in Carey Street was built in 1901 near the "dip" in Stamford Road. He had formed the business with his brother Harry in 1895, beginning in Wellington Street before brief spells in premises in School Lane and Northall Street. The Carey Street works were still in operation when the founder died in 1958 at the age of 90. To survive, the company entered into several mergers, from Mobbs Bros of Durban Road (1962) and Shire Shoes of Stamford Road (1966) to Coles of Burton Latimer (1974). By 1980 the company employed 500 workers at Carey Street and its sister factory, the Avondale Works in Connaught Street. There was a final merger with two Leicester firms, Gidley Wright and Diana Shoemakers, before the company crashed with debts of more than £1.4 million in 1982. A receiver was called in and the two Kettering factories went into liquidation with the loss of more than 300 jobs, but its third plant in Alexandra Road, Burton Latimer was saved by a consortium of three former managers. This finally succumbed in 1995 with 62 redundancies. The Carey Street premises were last occupied by wire manufacturers Percy Hawkins and Son. (*Evening Telegraph*)

As a junior reporter I covered several retirements and long-service presentations at the old Walker Last factory in Northall Street, pictured here in 1982 when lack of orders forced the firm into voluntary liquidation with the loss of 50 jobs. Its managing director since 1948 had been Charles Walker who, in his younger days, teamed up with Horace Hughes of Geddington as The Banjo Twins. He went on to form his own 16-piece dance band and played the double bass and guitar in the orchestra the night the Central Hall opened. He died in 1989, aged 79. The factory site, at the junction with Lower Street, is now occupied by the Windsor Gardens complex, consisting of 70 one- and two-person homes for the elderly. (*Frank Corvesor*)

CENTENARY
Evening Telegraph
100 YEARS OF NEWSPAPERS
1897 - 1997

EVENING
Telegraph

Dryland Street (formerly Workhouse Lane) was the ancestral home of the *Evening Telegraph* for almost 80 years. The Victorian three-storey-building, just beyond Dalkeith Shoes in this view, became the paper's first headquarters in 1897 and there it remained until the move to a new plant in Northfield Avenue in 1976. Right up until the 1970s, six district editions of the *ET* were printed here every day, plus the *Sports Telegraph* (nicknamed *The Pink 'Un*) on Saturdays during the football season. Each Friday its series of sister weekly papers would also roll off the huge presses which, in later years, printed such diverse publications as *Motor Cycle News*, *The Teacher* and *New Musical Express*. Dryland Street holds many memories for me of my first five years on the *ET* – days when it was produced by the old-fashioned "hot metal" process and reporters still bashed their stories out on antique-looking typewriters. Indeed, my first ever story in print was the theft of my own bicycle from outside the Dryland Street offices on my first day! The *ET* celebrated its centenary in 1997 and I felt proud and privileged when asked to research and write the paper's official 60-page birthday supplement. The following year, of course, the *ET* moved to new purpose-built premises in Rothwell Road, producing each issue with the latest state-of-the-art computer technology. A far cry from the battered black Olivetti typewriter I used as a cub reporter! (*Evening Telegraph*)

3. Kettering in Colour

Parish Church.

High Street.

Gold Street.

Greetings from Kettering

Geddington Cross.

Market Place.

Rushton Hall.

Kettering has enjoyed a colourful history and it seems appropriate to begin this chapter with a greetings card welcoming the reader to a unique glimpse into the town's past. I am delighted and deeply grateful that my publisher, Robert Wharton, has allowed me the luxury of reproducing the next few pages – and the subsequent chapter showcasing the late Frank Corvesor's work – in full colour. I have waited almost a decade for the chance to show off my small but impressive collection of hand-coloured postcards, most of them originally published between 1905 and the outbreak of World War I in 1914. Each photograph is evocative of its era and exudes an artistic quality of its own. Like a landscape painting, some of these pictures can only be truly appreciated when enlarged for optimum effect. As such, without wishing to sound pretentious, I consider them works of art in their own right, there to be admired, requiring little explanation from myself. That is why some of the captions are deliberately kept to a minimum. (*Tony Smith*)

Kettering Liberal Club, seen in all its glory on the right of this vivid view of Dalkeith Place circa 1908. Built of Weldon stone and red brick, it was erected in 1889 at a cost, including site, of £3,400. (*Tony Smith*)

No colour section on Kettering would be complete without the classic view of the Market Place, dominated by the magnificent spire of the parish church, the town's oldest building. This was taken in 1908 and it is not difficult to see why this scene has appeared on so many subsequent picture postcards. (*Tony Smith*)

A rare view of the parish church and library taken from the top of Station Road. Despite its 1913 postmark, the Alfred East Art Gallery, opened in July that year, does not feature. In those days the George Hotel, seen on the corner of Northampton Road, stretched almost the length of Sheep Street. The white sign proudly declares: "Hunting and livery stables. Horses and carriages on hire". (*Tony Smith*)

A fine close-up of the library, taken around 1910, three years after the Dryland Memorial was erected outside. A group of boys can be seen posing at one of the troughs. Fuller details on the library appear on page 10. (*Tony Smith*)

You won't see a better advert for nostalgia than this delightful picture looking up Gold Street around 1911, the year of George V's coronation (note the flying of the Union Jack). On the immediate left, next to the old terracotta Post Office buildings, are the old Crown Inn and Victoria Hall (the building with two gas lamps outside). In the distance is Fuller Chapel. (*Tony Smith*)

A rare postcard showing Kettering High Street from the direction of Gold Street in the early 1900s. On the left we see the old offices of Kettering Gas Company, with three gas lamps hanging over the window. The horse and carriage stands outside the Old White Horse Hotel (now Burtons menswear) and the group of people on the right are outside Woolworth's. (*Tony Smith*)

This postcard of High Street, taken from the direction of Market Place, was one of the first I ever purchased. A second copy, with the inscription "Happy New Year" across the sky, has been framed and hangs in my living room. Immediately recognisable on the right is the frontage of the former Northants Union Bank (now NatWest) and the spired building is the Old White Horse Hotel again. The postmark is 1923, but the picture was probably taken before World War I. (*Tony Smith*)

Station Road, 1907. (*Tony Smith*)

Kettering Library, circa 1905. (*Tony Smith*)

Kettering General Hospital, 1905. (*Tony Smith*)

Piccadilly Buildings, Sheep Street, 1930s. (*Tony Smith*)

I love this terrific view of Market Place, taken from the first floor of Lloyds Bank at the bottom of Market Street in the early 1930s. Facing the Royal Hotel is the old Boots store and Westminster Bank, whilst in the distance is the former Albion Temperance Hotel on Market Hill and one of the first Leyland Titan double-decker buses used by United Counties, seen passing the George Hotel in Sheep Street. (*Robert Wharton*)

One of the standard views looking up Gold Street from Bakehouse Hill, showing Brake's, the jewellers and pawnbrokers, in the 1920s. There was a famous burglary at Brake's on Thursday, 3 February 1921, discovered by Mr Brake himself when he happened to visit the premises at 9pm. One of the iron bars protecting the pledge office had been sawn off, and watches, brooches, bracelets and rings valued at £500 were missing. Police were called and Sgt Clarke went to the railway station after witnesses reported seeing two suspicious-looking strangers leave on the 8.48pm train for London. Insp. Brittain rang Scotland Yard at once and one man was seized in the subway at St Pancras station. The other bolted after throwing off his coat, found to have much of the loot in its pockets. The man was later apprehended, brought before Kettering Police Court the following Monday and sent to prison along with his accomplice. (*Tony Smith*)

I took this photograph in 1998 from the same place as the previous picture to allow comparison of the two. The front cover of my last book, *The Kettering Album*, shows the same scene yet again, captured by Frank Corvesor in 1960. It is interesting to note that the premises on the corner of Meeting Lane have always been occupied by jewellers. I'll leave you to decide which view is more pleasing to the eye. (*Tony Smith*)

Carey Baptist Church, on the corner of Nelson Street and King Street, celebrated its centenary in 1994. It was originally formed as a branch of Fuller Baptist Church to mark the centenary of the Baptist Missionary Society and as a memorial to William Carey, the famous former shoemaker who became its first missionary. The new mission, with the Reverend David John as its first minister, was deliberately set up in a part of Kettering where there was no church. Members met in a hall initially known as Nelson Street Chapel, but a new building was erected in 1911 at a cost of £3,500, with the Reverend John laying one of the foundation stones. Fuller donated the pulpit and organ and the church, seating 800 persons, was the first to be built without pillars to support the balcony. During World War II the hall was the venue for the Anglo-German Fellowship when many captured Germans were held at a PoW camp at Weekley. To commemorate the bicentenary of the Baptist Missionary Society in 1992 a special service at Carey Church was broadcast live by Anglia Television. (*Tony Smith*)

One of Kettering's most distinctive buildings is the Buccleuch Hotel on the corner of Stamford Road and Barnwell Street. Its most striking feature is its unusual spire, reminiscent of a fairytale castle from an old Walt Disney film. In 1891, when the hotel was built, the site was as far as Kettering stretched eastwards. It offered a limited number of bedrooms but its ample stabling, coach house and garage made it a popular and convenient place for huntsmen to stay in the early part of the century. It boasted a large and pleasant lawn at the rear, sheltered by trellis work, where customers could enjoy their drinks in the summer. The hotel also had an extensive kitchen garden where it grew its own vegetables, and a large upstairs function room for benefit concerts and other social events. Its genial host prior to World War I was Mr W. Norton of Cranford, previously proprietor of The Red Cow at Burton Latimer for 14 years. He was ably assisted by his daughter, who hunted with the Woodland Pytchley Hounds. An advertisement of the era boasted: "Our smoke-rooms are well patronised by all classes and all liquors are of the best quality, this being a free house for everything but draught ale." (*Tony Smith*)

To close this chapter we revert to the present day for this view of 1990s Kettering High Street, taken on a quiet Sunday lunchtime showing the Next fashion store sandwiched between the Etam ladieswear shop and Our Price records. The reason for including this particular photograph is to compare this part of the pedestrianised town centre with the picture on the opposite page, taken just over two decades ago. (*Tony Smith*)

4. The Corvesor Collection

Between 1958 and 1983 the late Frank Corvesor, co-founder of Dalkeith Ironmongers, took a series of colour transparencies in and around Kettering town centre. This chapter is devoted to this unique pictorial record, which shows much better than words the many changes brought about by the central area development scheme and the full impact on the town by the building of the Newborough Centre (now Newlands). This first picture from August 1977 was taken in the days when Tesco had shops in the High Street. A year later this branch became the first victim of the supermarket price war in Kettering. The shop had only 1,000 sq ft of space compared with Tesco's other developments in Wellingborough (20,000 sq ft) and Weston Favell (60,000 sq ft). Twenty-four jobs were lost, some transferring to other branches, and the premises were taken over by Birmingham-based newsagents Alf Preedy and Son. Tesco came to Kettering in the early 1960s as part of company expansion plans which also saw a £40,000 store open in Market Street, Wellingborough. (*Frank Corvesor*)

High Street

The final curve of Kettering High Street looking towards the old Grammar School and the Crown Inn in Gold Street, taken in March 1962.
To help get your bearings, Abbey National now occupies the right-hand site comprising Parkers and Calton and Nanette Shoes.
These were days when you could park in the town centre (see Mini van and signs). To the left, of course, is Bakehouse Hill, demolished in 1969
under town centre redevelopment. (*Frank Corvesor*)

An alternative look at the same row of shops as seen from Bakehouse Hill. The premises of cooked meat specialist Ernest Lewin (now further
down on the corner of Crispin Place) and Sharman and Son are now occupied by the trendy shoe shop Bon Marche, and Norvic is now part of
Waterstones book shop, which opened in 1997. (*Frank Corvesor*)

A view of Horsemarket and Dalkeith Place on a sunny September day in 1963 when Alexander Sloan occupied the former Cross Keys Restaurant. The building (now O'Malleys, an Irish theme pub) became the Jubilee Shopping Arcade, opened on 13 June 1977, so called because it was the year of the Queen's Silver Jubilee. Owned by the Nottingham-based firm Medidrive and managed by John Kitchen, this was an indoor market where up to 30 traders paid rent from £20 a week. Goods sold included fashion wear, haberdashery, curtains, fancy goods, pottery and glassware. All traders agreed to operate identical hours, from 9am to 5pm daily, except Thursday and Sunday. The shadow on the road is from the old Parish Church School. (*Frank Corvesor*)

Kettering High School

The old Kettering High School (now the council offices) pictured in July 1964, shortly before moving to a new site in Lewis Road (now Southfield School for Girls). The Bowling Green Road building, designed by John Alfred Gotch, was built by the county council to house 200 boys from the old Grammar School in Gold Street and a similar number of girls attending the newly-created High School. After an 11-year delay, classes began in 1913 under the respective headships of Mr John Irwin Scott and Miss Edith Bristol. From the first day, no contact was allowed between the boys and girls. The Grammar School moved to its new building in Windmill Avenue a year before this picture was taken. (*Frank Corvesor*)

Gold Street

A photograph of the upper stretch of Gold Street, also from 1964. As can be seen from the road markings at the traffic lights, motorists could not only use Gold Street but could choose to turn left into Newland Street, right into Silver Street or straight ahead into Montagu Street! The picture also shows the former Fuller Assembly Rooms to the left of the chapel, built in 1869 but demolished in 1977 to make way for the new Boots store in the Newborough Centre. Occupying its ground floor were Johnson's ladieswear shop and F. A. Coles, jewellers, the latter closing in 1976 after more than 40 years' trading and transferring its business to the firm's other shop further down on the other side of the street. (*Frank Corvesor*)

A motorist crosses the Gold Street crossroads in June 1967 passing Milletts' former shop (now the Texas Grill and Pancake House) and the fashion store Jax of London (now the Sense charity shop). Frames Tours can just be seen next door in Newland Street, and on the right is Paul Taylor's TV shop on the corner of Silver Street and Montagu Street (now Simpson and Partners, estate agents).
Paul, who died the year after this picture was taken aged 75, was Kettering's radio pioneer and the first in town to own a wireless. He was also a local councillor in the 1930s and a past president of Kettering Rotary Club. While his father Harry was building up his bicycle business (on the same Silver Street corner), Paul set up the first radio receiving station in Kettering using a simple crystal set. He started selling radio apparatus from his father's shop shortly before broadcasting began in 1922 and took over the business when his father died in 1932. Incredibly, six years later, using some early receivers, he gave demonstrations of crude TV pictures for the first time in Kettering. Paul Taylor and Partners were eventually taken over by York and Sons. Paul was a founder member of the Radio Traders' Retail Association (a national body) and belonged to the Royal Photographic Society. (*Frank Corvesor*)

Gold Street

Scaffolding in Gold Street, as the controversial Newborough Centre begins to take shape in March 1976. On the left is Sainsburys, which later moved into a new £326,000 store in the new complex. Its Gold Street self-service supermarket had been the first new building in Kettering's central development area and part of the "new look" town centre. Lord Sainsbury himself welcomed the first customers on 26 October 1965. Boasting a staff of 75, the 5,500 sq ft premises on the site of the old Crown Brewery introduced many new lines such as household goods, frozen foods, bread, fresh fruit and vegetables. Eight "checkouts" were introduced to avoid queues in a new five-day trading week, closing on Mondays but with longer hours on most other days. First in the queue on opening day was Rosa Smith of Lime Road, who had also been first customer when Boots opened its new High Street store four years earlier! (*Frank Corvesor*)

We move on to August 1977 for another glimpse of Gold Street showing F. A. Coles the jewellers (later Ratners, now H. Samuel) and the fashion shop Michael Anthony (with the Victorian-style window front). The latter closed the following month after 11 years in the town, when owner Tony Kay quit the retail business to concentrate on a new transport company formed with his wife Maureen. The shop (on the old site of Gerard's newsagents) first traded under the name Young Executive, branched out into women's fashions in 1973 and for a while had a branch in Market Harborough. Tony, a former president of Kettering Chamber of Trade, died of a heart attack in 1983, aged just 44. His premises were taken over by Jim Sterling, who ran the shoe shop pictured next door.
(*Frank Corvesor*)

This picture was taken on the same day as the Sainsburys shot on the previous page but lower down Gold Street to give a view of that giant crane which became such a fixture on the town's skyline for so long. Today none of these businesses remains in these premises. At the time of writing, Sainsburys was occupied by Mackays, the Electricity showrooms by Hamells ladieswear, Bennett the butchers became Palmers, Dolcis shoes were replaced by K. K. Books and Allans bakery and coffee lounge by the Norwich and Peterborough Building Society. (*Frank Corvesor*)

THE ROYAL, The Leading Family and Commercial Hotel of Kettering.

'BUSSES MEET THE TRAINS. HUNTING AND LIVERY STABLES. COVERED IN GARAGE.
Telephone No. 462.

The Royal Hotel has had a chequered history dating back to coaching days when it was known as the White Hart. Its name was changed in 1844 following the famous visit by Queen Victoria and Prince Albert en route to Stamford. It was rebuilt in 1878, and then the owner, the Duke of Buccleuch, sold it to brewers Pickering, Phipps and Co in 1896. The building is rich in architectural features, including an oriel window reminiscent of Kirby Hall. It also boasts a former billiard room handsomely panelled in walnut, which was turned into a carvery in 1979 as part of a £200,000 redesign (one of my claims to fame is playing the very last game of snooker there before the two full-size tables were removed!). The following year a planned £2 million revamp by owners Alney (UK) to bring the hotel up to four-star status, including the building of a swimming pool in the car park, never got off the ground. Sadly, another controversial scheme converting part of the premises into a new short-lived but appropriately named disco bar called The Bitter End did go ahead, leading to the controversial removal of the fine Victorian front window pictured here in 1982. Since then the hotel has had a succession of owners (one of which incurred the wrath of Kettering Civic Society by changing its historic name to The Perequito – apparently some kind of yellow parrot!). Strangely none of the Royal's encumbents over the years has thought to capitalise on its association with writer Charles Dickens, who stayed there whilst reporting a rather riotous by-election in 1835.
(*Frank Corvesor*)

Kettering's other long-established town centre hotel, the George, features in this photograph taken from the Market Place in July 1962. At that time Jewers' garage, complete with old-style petrol pumps, was still there, sandwiched between the Cherry Tree and Ainsworth's fish shop (later Mobbs'). The George Hotel had a seventeenth-century kitchen block, cellars even older, an eighteenth-century Georgian wing and a "Regency" room built in 1925. A new Coronation wing, designed by Gotch and Saunders, opened in 1954, boasting a new entrance hall, ground floor bar and 17 bedrooms, bringing the total to 48. Then in 1975, when Richard Smithson was manager, owners Paten Hotels gave the hotel a £100,000 facelift, replacing the old Coronation Bar with the new Dekker Bar, named after a seventeenth-century playwright who wrote The Shoemaker's Holiday. When this picture was taken, the manager was Fred Sykes, who retired in 1966 after 21 years in the job. He moved to North Wales but soon tired of retirement and in January 1967 became manager of a Coventry hotel, returning to Kettering with wife Babs as holiday relief at the George in August that year. (*Frank Corvesor*)

Local people under the age of 30 may be surprised to learn there used to be a school in the town centre dating back to 1873. Pictured here in Horsemarket in 1964 is the former Boys' National School, later known as the Parish Church School, a mixed secondary modern. The original building and Master's House, costing around £1,500, were erected by Charles Sharman on land donated by the Duke of Buccleuch. Made of red brick with stone framework for the Gothic-style windows, it initially catered for 200 boys up to the age of 13, funded mainly by voluntary subscriptions and a fee of a penny a week per pupil. Classes transferred to the Toller Sunday Schools while alterations were carried out in 1905 by Kettering builders C. and F. Henson. Its name changed to the Parish School in 1927 when girls were first admitted. They came from the Church Walk Infants' and Market Hill Girls' School, whose buildings were no longer considered adequate. (*Frank Corvesor*)

By the late 1950s pupil numbers at the Parish Church School, pictured here from London Road in June 1964, had risen to almost 300 and it became increasingly obvious that the building was outdated, overcrowded and badly sited. Desks were too small, the busy main road a constant danger to the children, and even the headmaster described the building as a "museum piece". Work began in February 1963 on a new school at the far end of Headlands, catering for up to 400 pupils, which became Bishop Stopford when it opened two years later. The derelict Horsemarket building, which had separate playgrounds and entrances for girls and boys, was finally demolished in September, 1970. (*Frank Corvesor*)

Horsemarket

Work on a new junction scheme for the top of Market Street and Horsemarket in 1975 meant the demolition of the surrounding wall to the former Parish Church School site. For more than a decade this land was used as a convenient but neglected town centre car park. Following motorists' complaints about its pot-holed condition, the council spent £12,000 resurfacing and landscaping the 1,075 square yard site, creating 14 short-stay parking spaces and room for trees to be planted. Four years later it became a taxi rank and remained so until 1999 when, under the new town centre revamp, it was grassed over and landscaped. (*Frank Corvesor*)

The corner of the Parish Church School can just be glimpsed in this picture of Horsemarket, taken from the top of Market Street in June 1966. Menswear store Roadnights, which later moved to Lower Street, was the place to shop when I was a fashion-conscious young reporter in the early 1970s (if you liked pink loon pants, red velvet flares, loud round-collared Brutus shirts and floral ties, that is). The *ET* also made us hire formal evening suits from here when covering dinner-dances at Wicksteed Park because they were cheaper than Burtons! (*Frank Corvesor*)

This view of the High Street was taken in July 1967 – the year of flower power, the summer of love, the height of the Swinging Sixties (man!). Kettering trendsetters had a choice of Foster Bros (cheap and cheerful) and Dunn and Co (if you wanted tweeds and a nice trilby). Sandwiched between the two was one of Kettering's long-established and best-loved shops, J. C. Bond. They described themselves as stationers, but here you could also buy books, fancy goods, crested china and toys, from various floors. In their early days, Bonds even published their own picture postcards of Kettering and at Christmas had a rival Santa to the one upstairs in Currys. The company was sold to Birmingham-based firm Alfred Preedy in November 1978 shortly after the same firm moved into Tesco's old premises in High Street. Staff were assured the store would not close as a result of the £3.4 million takeover, but the writing was on the wall and in 1982 the premises were taken over by Apple, the arts, crafts and gift shop. It is now a charity shop for the Imperial Cancer Research Fund. (*Frank Corvesor*)

75

We now move further along High Street (and a decade later than the previous page) to the bottom of Dryland Street in August 1977, the year of the Queen's Silver Jubilee. Here, local ladies could tog up for their street party from dear old Dorothy Perkins. As you can see, the shop was up for let in anticipation of moving into the Newborough Centre, the construction of which is taking place to the far left of the picture. The vacated premises were taken over by menswear store Mr Howard, later to become Mr Goodbuy. Several tenants later, it is the home of health food store Holland and Barratt. Allans cake shop next door is now Buckinghams. (*Frank Corvesor*)

Del Boy seems to have left his yellow Robin Reliant in Kettering High Street in this interesting photograph from 1977. Just ahead in the distance, next to Wigfalls, is the old Boots store before the chemists moved into much larger premises in the Newborough Centre. Boots moved to High Street from the bottom of Market Street in 1961 as part of the company's £10 million five-year shop development plan, modernising 94 of its branches. The new £43,000 self-service store was built on the site of the old Gaumont Pavilion cinema, which was demolished in July 1960. The new three-storey building was five times bigger than the Market Street store. There were two large sales floors and the top storey was used for stock and staff rooms. I remember they had those really tacky framed prints on the walls as you went upstairs, but most exciting for us kids was the new gramophone department on the first floor, where I purchased my first Beatles singles, after listening to them in a soundproof booth – a first for Kettering! The store officially opened its doors on 17 November 1961, and heading the queue (surprise, surprise) was Kettering's shopaholic Rosa Smith (no relation), who bought hand-conditioning cream for 1s. 6d. (7p) and was given a free leather shopping bag worth £3. 9s. 6d. (£3.47). To the right of Boots in the picture is the Leicester Building Society (now Alliance and Leicester, of course) and Civils supermarket and wine store, which closed down in August 1980 because of the disposal of the lease and was replaced by Dixons. The old Boots premises are currently occupied by Superdrug. (*Frank Corvesor*)

Dalkeith Ironmongers

A striking picture of the rather spectacular awning outside Dalkeith Ironmongers in Horsemarket, taken in May 1978 by the man who co-founded the firm back in 1936. In 1922 the late Frank Corvesor, whose historic photographs fill this chapter, travelled from Bridgnorth in Shropshire to work as an apprentice ironmonger for his cousin, Robert Bell at the bottom of Bakehouse Hill, Kettering (as pictured on page 7). There he met Ernest Lillyman, who had joined the firm three years earlier, but neither dreamed this would be the start of a long and happy partnership. Their first shop, simply called Lillyman and Corvesor, opened in Market Street three years before the outbreak of World War II. They took over the Horsemarket premises after the war and their friendly service and expert advice were appreciated by customers, many travelling from other towns, for more than three decades. They took particular pride in the knowledge that if you couldn't get what you wanted in their store, you were unlikely to get it anywhere else in the town. (*Frank Corvesor*)

Frank Corvesor and Ernest Lillyman pictured in their Horsemarket store in October 1980. With Mr Corvesor (left) in his 70s and Mr Lillyman in his 80s, they both decided it was time to retire and handed down the business to their respective sons, Leo and Richard. But times were changing in the hardware trade, and within the next decade DIY superstores were springing up everywhere, combining larger stock and competitive prices with quick and easy parking. The firm finally succumbed to the recession in 1992, its premises taken over by Newlec Cycles, which itself closed in 1998. Mr Corvesor, a keen gardener as well as photographer, died after a short illness in October 1987, aged 81. (*Leo Corvesor*)

The Victorian block of three shops on the corner of High Street and Wadcroft, pictured in August 1977, when it was occupied by Falfords newsagents (with the dodgy sign), Halfords motor accessories store and Branhills dress shop. The building, owned by the Kettering Old Grammar School Foundation, was demolished in July 1979 and replaced with a new block with brick facing and slate roof, designed by Gotch, Saunders and Surridge. It was a vast improvement to the look of the High Street, and service access was to the rear. All three shops eventually moved out, the last to go being Halfords, which took over the former James Brothers store in Gold Street (smaller premises) in September 1978. Timpsons shoe shop later took over the corner block, with furnishers Cavendish Woodhouse, whose lease on its Silver Street premises had expired, moving in next door. Halfords' old store became Preedy's, the newsagents, tobacconists and booksellers. (*Frank Corvesor*)

London Road

The junction of St Mary's Road with London Road as it was in July 1961, before traffic lights were introduced and London Road widened accordingly, the extra lane robbing the corner of its fence-ringed grass verge. When the new traffic system came into force in February 1973, two large new road signs were erected outside St Edward's Church (just out of picture on left), causing consternation among Kettering Civic Society members, who described them as "hideous monstrosities" and a waste of public money. As a compromise they were repositioned on either side of the church front. (*Frank Corvesor*)

Another London Road picture from 1961 shows the row of old stone cottages almost facing St Mary's Hospital, which were pulled down by Kettering Council just a few years later. The terraced houses, extending from Wallis's garage in the distance, dated from the Victorian era and bore a plaque inscribed "Prospect Place, J. J., 1847". These were the initials of the Reverend John Jenkinson, a pastor who came to Kettering from Hallaton in 1822 and built his own church, Ebenezer Chapel, just off Silver Street (it later became a factory which was eventually demolished, but the name Ebenezer Place remains). He had a market garden in Meeting Lane, where his name lives on in Jenkinson's Block. In 1967 Prospect Place made way for Harry Potter House, a new block of 20 old people's flatlets costing £46,000 and named after the long-serving councillor. (*Frank Corvesor*)

A lovely view from 1964 of the original Corn Market Hall and its neighbouring pig pens in the old cattle market in London Road. It was erected by the urban council in 1913 at a cost of £1,300 and used on market days by local corn merchants, millers and farmers who met there. Built of Duston stone with a blue slate roof, it was officially opened by Cllr Henry Barlow and was hired out for bazaars, household sales, auctions and public meetings. During World War II it was in continuous use by the Women's Voluntary Service as a recreation room and canteen for soldiers (a commemorative plaque still hangs in the main hall). After the war it had a variety of uses, including a school gymnasium and council chamber. Renovations began in 1987 to alter and upgrade the building at a cost of £225,000, and it was re-opened on 4 May 1988 by Mayor Cllr Ken Gosland, winning Kettering Civic Society's Silver Rose Bowl for its contribution to the local environment. The main hall now seats up to 200 people, complete with a kitchen, licensed bar and galley, and there is an extension at the back housing another four meeting rooms. Much of the building's original materials were re-used and there is a new entrance, with disabled access, from the car park. (*Frank Corvesor*)

Market Street

The top of Market Street pictured in May 1970 before the installation of traffic lights and the alterations to its junction with London Road and Horsemarket. In earlier years, Clarksons, on the corner, was the unofficial "tuck shop" for pupils from the old Parish Church School opposite. The corner premises are now occupied by Keeble and Son, the estate agents and valuers, and the old terraced house next door (No. 4 London Road) is used by Victim Support, a group which helps victims of crime. Those who bought my last book, *The Kettering Album*, may like to compare this picture with the Victorian view on page 10. (*Frank Corvesor*)

London Road

It's funny how the memory plays tricks on you. Before I saw this 1967 picture of London Road, I could have sworn the town's old police station was on the same spot as its replacement (next to Church Walk, where the bollards are). But, as seen here, the station was a few hundred yards to the right, where part of the courthouse and probation offices now stand. The present police headquarters are sited on the vacant land behind the lamppost and old bus stop in this photograph.
(*Frank Corvesor*)

The town's old police station in London Road in April 1967 not long before it was demolished. After being partially rebuilt in 1909, it was regarded by architects as one of the best-looking police stations in the country. The frontage was in the early Victorian style, some 182ft in length (80ft of which was occupied by the previous building). In those days the ground floor housed the female witnesses' room, two courts and magistrates' retiring room to the rear, a guard room and inspector's house (with men's quarters on the first floor). The main station and courthouse entrance door was made of oak and the building also housed two new cells (replacing two old ones), a mess room, kitchen and larder. Its eventual £120,000 replacement opened in October 1969 just as demolition work began on the old, and by then, shabby and decaying building.

(Frank Corvesor)

Carey Mission House

Now for two interesting pictures of ancient Kettering buildings, only one of which survives. On the right is the Carey Mission House, historic home of the Baptist Missionary Society, pictured in January 1965. The plaque embedded in the front hedge tells the story of how this spectacular seven-bayed house in Lower Street, the home of Martha Wallis, became the society's birthplace following a meeting there in 1792. The building was converted into flats for the elderly by the Baptist Housing Association in 1974 and a later complex of 32 self-contained flats built behind the Mission House was named Martha Wallis Court. Silhouetted against the skyline in this picture is the malting tower of the old Elworthy brewery, which closed in 1931. (*Frank Corvesor*)

Beech House

The front porch and garden of Beech House in old Tanners Lane, acquired by Kettering Council in 1971 and pictured here on a sunny day in September 1973, two years before this fine listed building was demolished to make way for the Newborough Centre. It was one of the most contentious decisions in Kettering's more recent history, and only came about following a bitter struggle with local campaigners and an expensive public inquiry. Beech House dated from Queen Anne, the oldest part having been built in 1704. It was home to generations of well-known Kettering families, including the Wrights, Wallises, Butlins and Stockburns. (*Frank Corvesor*)

The shadow from Kettering's head post office stretches almost to the other side of Lower Street in this fascinating photo from June 1966. It shows the row of long-gone shops stretching to Bakehouse Hill before pedestrianisation. Next to Gaymoor, the ladies' hairdressers run by Vera Coleman, was Garley's cycle shop, one of Kettering's biggest success stories. The business was originally set up by Maurice Garley in Hampden Crescent during the 1930s but taken over by his brother Bert when he died. Bert, previously a plumber with Miller and Charles in Tresham Street, built up the business, selling tents and camping equipment to boy scouts from the second shop in Lower Street, as well as bicycles and accessories. In 1949 he opened two factories in Burton Latimer, one making cycle bags and leather shopping bags and the other branching out into children's playground equipment. By the end of the 1950s a third factory in Gretton was producing cycle shorts and vests while another in Finedon manufactured cycling shoes. A motor cycle shop which Bert took over in Regent Street added to this booming business, which exported goods all over the world, from Europe, Canada and the USA to Australia and New Zealand. When Bert died from cancer in 1967, aged 60, his wife Jessie kept the Kettering shops going, helped by daughter Sue, but sold up three years later. Two doors down in the photograph is the Halifax Building Society, now operating from the other side of Lower Street. (*Frank Corvesor*)

Market Street

Boots the Chemists' original shop at the bottom corner of Market Street in 1960, a year before its new premises were built in High Street (see page 77). This was an interesting building, dating back to the turn of the century. Its original lettering could still be seen etched on the glass windows and for many years it operated its own lending library upstairs. It was knocked down in the 1970s and is currently occupied by Barclays Bank. (*Frank Corvesor*)

Market Place

A view of Market Place looking back towards the Royal Hotel and Lloyds Bank in High Street in July 1963. On the corner of West Street is Poole's newsagents (now Totan's jewellers) next to land agents and surveyors Berry Bros and Bagshaw (now operating in Rockingham Road as Berry Bros and Holmes). Just in view is the awning of hairdressers and tobacconists Frank Page, which began in Northall Street back in the early part of the century. (*Frank Corvesor*)

A wonderful "olde worlde" view of Christopher Dixon's cobblers shop at the West Street junction with Hazelwood Lane, taken in July 1963. A drawing of this building by the late local artist C. Dudley Brown was issued as a Christmas card by Kettering Civic Society and also appeared on the front cover of Book One in Tony Ireson's excellent series *Old Kettering – A View From the 1930s*. The old building was bought by Kettering Council in 1959, demolished in 1972 and is now waste ground. It stood on the site of the old Nag's Head Inn, a popular public house during the eighteenth century, when West Street was called Nag's Head Lane. It later became known as Mr Lamb's Lane, as it ran from the former Turnpike Road (now Market Place) to Mr Lamb's premises at the bottom of the hill. To this day Lamb and Holmes' solicitors office remains in West Street. (*Frank Corvesor*)

Kettering Market

The hustle and bustle of Kettering Market, captured by Mr Corvesor's camera one sunny day in June 1966, the summer England won the World Cup! The old Corn Exchange, erected in 1853, is still the most imposing building overlooking the Market Place (apart from the parish church, of course). Its uses have ranged from council chamber and library to function hall and cinema (Vint's Electric Palace, later the Hippodrome, which closed in 1922). Kettering Council bought the Corn Exchange in 1926 to use as an indoor market and it has been occupied by various shops since (in this picture, Paulettes). John Blundell's store to the left is now Mister Ray, selling cut-price household goods. (*Frank Corvesor*)

A view of the market looking towards the church, taken on the same day. In 1977 the whole town came together to celebrate the 750th anniversary of the Market Charter. Festivities included an exhibition, a two-day cavalcade of entertainment by local people, and a medieval charity market at which the Mayor, Cllr Albert Morby, ceremonially read out the original royal charter. Many hundreds of people took part in a two-act history of Kettering in music, song and dance written and co-produced by the late Gladys Riseley, and performed over two nights at the Poppies ground. They represented more than 40 local schools, clubs, youth groups, bands, choirs and drama societies. (*Frank Corvesor*)

Blanchflowers was one of Kettering's long-established motor dealers and repairers, dating back to the early part of the century. Its Northfield garage and filling station, pictured here in 1961, was on the corner of Northampton Road and Northfield Avenue, a prime site for drivers coming in and out of Kettering on the A43. It opened in 1928 just as the motoring boom was beginning to take off and offered a complete motoring service, from engine overhauls to complete chassis and body rebuilding. As well as keeping a large stock of used cars, Blanchflowers could supply any make of car or commercial vehicle. When this photograph was taken, they were dealers for Humber, Hillman, Sunbeam, Wolseley and Renault and the following year sold and serviced Dodge, Commer and BMC vans after merging with A. W. H. Porter, who ran the Cresta Service Station in Burton Road, Finedon. In the late 1960s Blanchflowers took over premises in Newland Street (later Timberland) and ran a petrol station in Rockingham Road, after the compulsory purchase of its Northfield garage for the town's proposed western relief road. When nothing came of this proposal the derelict building became a major eyesore throughout the 1970s. Part of the site fronting Northfield Avenue was turned into the ATS tyre and exhaust depot in 1983, and three years later the site facing Northampton Road was demolished and replaced by the Elite showrooms, selling fridges, cookers, washing machines and other electrical goods. It is now Titles video store. (*Frank Corvesor*)

Meadow Road

The top of Meadow Road at its junction with High Street in 1969, when International Stores (originally International Tea Stores) still occupied the corner premises (now McDonalds). For 60 years this site was Jones's grocery and wine stores, but deeds showed that the actual shop premises went back to 1770 when there was a pond at the junction. International Stores took over in 1932, and from 1933 to 1973 the manager was Leslie Dayman, whose wife Phyllis had been his assistant from 1939. In the early years, when Meadow Road was still called Gas Street, everything had to be weighed and packed by staff in the shop. The branch closed in February 1984 after failing to find new and larger premises to compete with rival supermarkets in Kettering.
(*Frank Corvesor*)

The same section of Meadow Road looking up from the direction of Commercial Road. For many years the white buildings were rented by solicitors Wilson and Wilson (now Wilson Browne) until taken over by Marks and Spencer in 1969, enabling the store to expand its ground floor space by 50 per cent. Wilson and Wilson moved into a new purpose-built four-storey building lower down Meadow Road (opposite the Talbot Hotel). Its senior partner at that time was Mr P. T. M. (Peter) Wilson, who in 1976 completed 50 years' service with the firm formed by his father at the end of the last century. Peter, a former president of Kettering Caledonian Society, became chairman of the Northampton-based Anglia Building Society in 1970, and from 1957 to 1973 chaired Northamptonshire Newspapers, which owned the *Evening Telegraph* and its weekly papers. He died in 1986, aged 82, two years after retiring. (*Frank Corvesor*)

I wonder how many readers can remember Meadow Road (then Gas Street) when it was little more than a narrow lane, as seen here looking up from the direction of Northfield Avenue in May 1958. The long wall and old buildings on the right, which included a row of terraced homes, disappeared when the road was widened in the 1960s. They were replaced by the new Wilson and Wilson solicitors' offices and Sir John Brown Court, a complex of flats for retired ex-servicemen and women or widows of ex-servicemen, named after a prominent member of the British Legion (I covered its official opening for the *Evening Telegraph* in 1972). On the left are the old gas company offices (now Transco), part of the sprawling gasworks site totalling 2.9 acres. The giant gas holder (100ft high and 138ft in diameter), erected at the turn of the century, was no longer needed after the conversion to North Sea gas, and its remaining steel shell was finally dismantled in 1975, its site now occupied by B & Q and Comet. Top left of the picture is the Talbot Hotel, run at that time by Fred and Doris Hefford, who took over as landlord and landlady on 8 September 1948 and went on to celebrate 21 years behind the bar in 1969. Former shoeworker Fred, vice-chairman of Kettering's Licensed Victuallers Association, was a boxing lover who trained local fighters, whilst wife Doris used to sew buttons on to Co-op Society clothing. (*Frank Corvesor*)

Newland Street

Newland Street, pictured in June 1960, when two-way traffic was allowed. On the corner of Montagu Street (now Bairstow Eves, estate agents) was Woodcocks, the drapers, furnishers and milliners. The firm was founded in 1894 by Ernest Woodcock, a Kettering councillor from 1912 to 1928 (chairman in 1922) and county councillor, who was made Alderman in 1938. Ernest, a former chairman of Kettering Chamber of Trade, was the first Kettering shopkeeper to have incandescent lighting outside his premises. The store always had a splendid stock of ladieswear, hats, underwear, curtains and baby linen. When it closed in September 1960, son Alwyne Woodcock, who was born on the premises when the family also lived there, was managing director and his brother Douglas was director. The store, which had expanded over the years, was taken over by Kettering Industrial Co-operative Society. (*Frank Corvesor*)

Newland Street was a little worse for wear when this picture was taken in 1967. Man Fung was Kettering's first Chinese restaurant, and the old Co-op and Labour Institute, a venue for countless functions since it opened in 1926, was demolished in 1981 because it was riddled with dry rot and deemed dangerous. These two buildings, plus Ken Burton's old sports shop on the left, sat on the site now occupied by the Fuller Coffee House.
(*Frank Corvesor*)

Another Newland Street picture from 1967, taken from the direction of Rockingham Road. All these premises, including popular pork butchers Peak Creasey (now the entrance to Newlands), were demolished to prepare land for Phase 3 of the Newborough Centre. The butchers, established for 40 years, were founded by William Peak Creasey, who was born in Timberland, Lincolnshire but came to Kettering as a boy. The self-proclaimed "sausage king", who died in 1944 aged 67, served on the council for many years and was president of Kettering Cage Bird Society, Kettering Rifle Band Club, and Kettering Darts League. He was also a Freemason and associated with Kettering Town Harriers. (*Frank Corvesor*)

The block of buildings at the junction of Newland Street and Northall Street in June 1983, where Iceland freezer centre now stands. I used to buy cheap second-hand records and comics from Clive Chester's fancy goods shop on the corner. Clive once offered old £1 notes for sale at £2 each to collectors ("Cheap at twice the price," he said). Next door was Roy Christie's bookmakers, a sister shop to the main business he founded in Montagu Street (next to Swinglers off-licence) in 1968. At one time Christie's (who later took over Yorks TV shop in Montagu Street where they remain today, managed by son John) owned 21 betting shops across the Midlands, including branches in Desborough, Rothwell and Burton Latimer. (*Frank Corvesor*)

Newland Street

A nostalgic view (right) of Newland Street and Rockingham Road in May, 1965, showing how narrow Northall Street used to be before it was widened for the inner ring road. Opposite the Sewing Machine Shop is Blackett's corner, a distinctive early Victorian building originally used as a bakehouse and shop, with the bakers living in the two adjoining houses. It was taken over by Mr Blackett in the early 1920s but eventually ceased bread-making to become a wine and spirit merchant. The building was demolished in 1966.
(*Frank Corvesor*)

The former KICS butchers shop on the corner of Newland Street and St Andrew's Street. When this was taken in January 1962, there was a row of terraced houses in Newland Street to the left of the Stag and Pheasant pub. Now called the Shire Horse, this is the building on the left beyond the street lamp, with a van parked outside. All these properties disappeared when the new inner ring road was opened in the 1970s and traffic lights now control the junction.
(*Frank Corvesor*)

A rare photograph of the former North End School, also known as the St Andrews Church Institute, in Northall Street in 1969. The single-storey brick building, almost opposite Jack Cross newsagents, was erected for 200 primary-age pupils in 1859. Complete with tall chimney stacks and a 30ft bell turret, it was designed by Edmund Law, the architect of the old Grammar School in Gold Street, and built by William Henson, whose other notable buildings included the Corn Exchange, Fuller Church and the old police station in London Road. In the early part of the century it was the venue for "Band of Hope" lantern lectures on the evils of drinking and smoking, with photographer Warren East operating the "magic lantern" projector, later resurrected by Fred Moore (see page 166). The L-shaped school building fell uncomfortably between two council projects in the 1970s – the Newborough Centre and the inner ring road. It had a temporary reprieve in April 1975 when Kettering Civic Society warned Whitehall that the bulldozers were moving in. An inspector was despatched to Kettering but concluded it was "not of sufficient merit" to be listed and preserved. With the school went the underground toilets with their distinctive Victorian-style green railings. (*Frank Corvesor*)

Northall Street

Jack Cross's newsagents and Central Printing Works pictured from North End School in March 1965. I remember interviewing Jack Cross jun., then 70, on his enforced retirement in 1974 when his shop was compulsorily purchased by Kettering Council to make way for the inner ring road. He was proud of working up to 95 hours a week, even in his 60s, to keep going the business started by his father, also Jack, shortly after the turn of the century. The council told Jack junior as far back as 1957 that land was required for the new road, and alternative accommodation was arranged across the road on the site of the Waggon and Horses public house. Plans were passed by the council, which then bought the shop, but they were shelved in 1961, by which time the cost of new premises had almost doubled. Jack went into partnership with his father just after World War II, taking over on his death in 1951. The Central Printing Works, rebuilt with a new warehouse in 1968, was sold to Surridge Dawson. (*Frank Corvesor*)

Richard Leys

The old British Legion headquarters in Richard Leys in June 1966. The corrugated iron building, one of the casualties of the new Sainsburys site a decade later, was the first permanent headquarters of the Kettering branch since it was formed in 1921. Members acquired the former billiards saloon in 1947, repairing and decorating the delapidated building, to be used for meetings, dances, jumble sales and other fundraising activities. It was on a prominent corner next to the Lindrea leather works (just in picture), which was gutted by fire in 1975. By then the factory was empty, having been bought by the council for town centre development. A new British Legion club was incorporated in the Newborough Centre.
(*Frank Corvesor*)

In Sheep Street, at the top of Station Road, stands a quaint and attractive building, the facade of which has remained virtually unaltered in more than 300 years. Pictured here in July 1963, Sawyer's Almshouses were originally built for six elderly women in 1688, the legacy of the seafaring merchant Edmund Sawyer. In his will, written aboard the Mediterranean trading ship Asia on 12 December 1887, he left £100 towards the building of "a hospital or house for the poor of Kettering". It was not until 1950 that Edmund's burial place was found in the Greek Orthodox Church at Alexandretta in Turkey. In 1960 the first major structural alterations were made when the trust responsible spent £2,106 converting the building to three houses using only the ground floor, each having a living room with electric cooker, small bedroom, kitchenette, bath and toilet (previously tenants shared one outside toilet). The work was carried out by Boughton Estates, which also paid £606 towards the cost. The almshouses, which have 21-inch walls, were further modernised in 1988 when Kettering Council backed an £80,000 renovation scheme. Sawyer's coat of arms, mounted above the front door, is pictured on page 1. (*Frank Corvesor*)

Northfield Avenue

The Northfield Avenue crossroads, with Rothwell Road to the left and Lower Street to the right, pictured in 1962. The scene was more rural then, with a clear view of the chimneys from Kettering furnaces, which closed in 1959 and were demolished a year after this was taken. Northfield Avenue, a mile-long, 50ft wide artery road from Northampton Road to Rockingham Road, was built by 100 men in 1925/26 at a cost of £21,000. At the time it was the largest scheme undertaken by Kettering Urban Council, being 100 yards longer than Windmill Avenue and a quarter of a mile longer than Gipsy Lane. In 1983 the stretch between the two railway bridges was widened and re-aligned at a cost of £320,000. Today this is a bustling roundabout dominated by the Do It All store on the far corner. (*Frank Corvesor*)

Manor House Gardens

A pleasant view of Kettering's Manor House gardens in bloom during May 1958, taken from the Headlands end of Sheep Street The parish church overlooks the Alfred East Gallery on the left and the Grammar School/High School building (now the council offices) is just visible on the far right. When the art gallery was built in 1913, the gardens were simply known as the Manor House field, used as the meeting place for large gatherings and the departure point for major parades and processions. (*Frank Corvesor*)

When this photograph was taken in Sheep Street in September 1963, I was still in short trousers, having celebrated my ninth birthday the previous month. It was from this very bus stop outside the art gallery that I would catch the 292 service back to my home in Elizabeth Road on the Grange Estate after shopping in town or returning my library books. In fact, before I passed my driving test in 1976, I was still an occasional United Counties passenger in the early 1970s, catching buses to meet girlfriends who lived in such remote jungles as Desborough or Little Harrowden. I was also an occasional commuter to the old *ET* offices in Dryland Street (getting off at the shelter in Horsemarket) when it was either too wet to walk or I was too lazy! Believe it or not, my first ever story for the paper in 1971 was the theft from work of the trusty bicycle which had got me safely to and from Kettering Grammar School for the previous six years. (*Frank Corvesor*)

Northampton Road

Until relatively recently the Northampton Road railway bridge, seen here from the town side in 1974, was a notorious accident blackspot. In 1962, 14 people were injured when it was struck by a double-decker bus and during the 1970s high-load lorries often got stuck or shed their loads. This problem was also experienced at the Rothwell Road bridge and became so common there that, before Do It All was built next to the *ET*, photographers could take pictures with a telephoto lens without needing to leave the office! (*Frank Corvesor*)

A view of the Northampton Road bridge from the other side, looking towards the town in 1966. Emergency repairs were needed in 1973 when the structure had become weak from being struck by too many lorry drivers who didn't seem to know the height of their own vehicles. Five years later the worst incident occurred – 30 children were injured when the roof of a double-decker bus from Coventry was ripped off like the lid of a sardine can. New computerised signs now forewarn and divert high vehicles as they approach both railway bridges in Kettering. (*Frank Corvesor*)

A moody shot of Lower Street in February 1961, showing a beat bobby (remember them?) crossing the zebra crossing from Blains, the London furriers, to the GPO, as it was then called. Blains, to the right of Garley's cycle shop (see colour picture on page 85), was run by brothers Maurice and Alan Bland, one of whom lived above the shop and the other commuted from London. The partners also wrote music together and several of their popular songs were published. After central redevelopment, the business (first established in London in 1908) moved to Rockingham Road, but eventually closed after being the target of anti-fur protestors. From the mid-1980s animal rights campaigners broke windows and daubed the building with paint. On 10 February 1990 more than 40 marchers left two coffins and several wreaths outside the shop because it was the last in the county to sell real fur coats. To the right of Blains in this picture is Leslie Smart's jewellers, first established at corner premises in Upper Street after World War II. When town centre redevelopment got under way, the firm moved from Lower Street to a more spacious shop in Gold Street (formerly Tilleys, the confectioners). Mr Smart, who learned his trade with Newland Street jeweller Walter U. Baker, died in April 1992 aged 79. Although he retired at 65, he regularly called into the shop to chat with customers. (*Frank Corvesor*)

Lower Street

The final photograph in this unique Frank Corvesor series is another 1961 view of Lower Street, snapped from the direction of High Street. This was taken after the Gaumont Pavilion cinema was demolished on the left but before the new Boots store was erected in its place (see page 77). Bell and Billows can just be seen on the right at the bottom of Bakehouse Hill. The last shop to go on Bakehouse Hill was Theobalds, which moved round the corner in August 1969 to join other shops in the new row of replacement shops in Lower Street. In the distance you can see the sign of the Peacock pub (left), Leslie Smart's shop (right) and the old brewery maltings (far right).
(*Frank Corvesor*)

5. At Your Service

As the title suggests, this chapter takes a look at some of the well-known Kettering shops and businesses which made their name through their quality and service to local customers. There can be no better example of this than Bagshaws Fish Restaurant (above) on the corner of Dryland Street and Dalkeith Place. It was the end of an era when this popular "chippie" closed on Wednesday, 22 June 1990 – 90 years after the family first set up shop in the town's Stamford Road. Brothers Barry, then 47, and John Bagshaw, 53, blamed spiralling rents and rates for the end of the business begun by their grandfather Jack at the turn of the century. Jack began selling poultry, pheasants, rabbits and potatoes but branched out into selling fried food and at one time the family owned four fish-and-chip shops in Kettering. Jack, who retired in 1943, was succeeded by son Edward, who began working with his father in 1924. Three generations of fish fryers were complete when Edward's own son John joined in 1956, followed three years later by younger brother Barry, then just 14. When the shop first opened, a bag of fish and chips cost 1s. 1d. (just over 5p) and during the last war the family got special consignments of oil to keep the shop open because it provided such a good and cheap meal (customers no doubt included impoverished young reporters from the nearby *ET* offices!) The bombshell was dropped in early 1990 when Bagshaws learned that their annual rent was to more than treble, from £10,000 to £33,000. At least the tradition continues – the premises at 27/28 Dalkeith Place are now occupied by the Tudor Fish Restaurant and Takeaway. (*Tony Smith*)

The Central Motor Company in Dalkeith Place were well-known agents for new cars and motor cycles, and also hired cars to the public. The petrol pump attendant in this marvellous 1930s photograph can be seen working a hand-operated pump to fill up the car standing on the forecourt near the Prince of Wales pub. Central Motors began in 1919 from small premises in Ebenezer Place, moving to Dalkeith Place the following year. The company opened a filling station in London Road, subsequently developed to accommodate coachbuilding and agricultural departments. I may not have been born if it hadn't been for Central Motors – it was where my late parents first met. My father Rodger was a mechanic there before entering the insurance business and mother Joan (née Hart) worked in the office. (*Tony Smith*)

Three smart Daimlers parked outside the Central Garage on Wednesday, 6 November 1935. They were used to ferry Royal passengers from Kettering Station to Boughton House following the wedding of the Duke of Gloucester, third son of the Queen, to Lady Alice Scott in the chapel at Buckingham Palace. Their train arrived in Kettering at 5pm, where the newlyweds were welcomed by urban council chairman, Cllr C Mayes, and other local dignitaries. The couple were then driven to their honeymoon "lodgings" in a partially-closed Daimler Landaulette, followed by the two other official cars carrying guests. More than 4,000 schoolchildren lined the streets at special roped-off vantage points, and the town's wedding gift was a set of four Georgian silver candlesticks, which had been on show all week in a window of Ernest Woodcock's store in Newland Street. (*Tony Smith*)

Pictured outside Central Motors in the 1940s is this intriguing wartime vehicle, complete with blackout lighting masks on its headlamps (probably used by the Home Guard). In 1961, the garage moved its head office and motor business to London Road, concentrating on the agricultural side at Dalkeith Place. The whole operation moved to London Road a year later when the company was taken over by Mr W. D. Evans of Burton Latimer. The Dalkeith Place premises were sold to motor body builders A. E. Smith in 1968, and Central's Volkswagen agency moved to its Darley Dale service station in Corby. This, and the London Road garage, were taken over by the Dutton Forshaw group in May, 1969 – ironically, the company's 50th anniversary year. (*Tony Smith*)

F. A. Watts

The frontage of the former F. A. Watts' furniture shop, next to the Post Office arcade in Gold Street, pictured in 1934, a year after moving from Goosey's old drapery premises in High Street (later the site of the Granada cinema, now a bingo hall). The family firm was founded by Arthur Watts, who opened his first shop in Adnitt Road, Northampton in 1896. The firm moved to two sites in the town's Kettering Road before settling in Abington Street in 1931 – the year Arthur died. The first Kettering branch, managed by Jack Thompson, had opened in 1923. Watts also had outlets in Wellingborough, first in Oxford Street and then Cambridge Street. (*Francis Watts*)

Watts employees pictured outside the Gold Street store before a staff coach trip in 1937. For many years the Kettering store provided furniture and rolls of lino for offices of Stuart and Lloyds (later British Steel) in Corby. The shop also provided a cabinet-making and upholstery service and, as an interesting sideline, sold prams and nursery equipment. In the 1930s three piece suites cost 19 guineas (the shop once sold 12 in one day) and you could buy a big wardrobe and dressing table for £9.19s.6d. A bedstead, which included the spring, was £3.19s.6d. (*Francis Watts*)

The management and employees of F. A. Watts prior to leaving for Hunstanton on Thursday, 21 June 1956. The excursion was to celebrate the firm's 60th year in business and was the first outing from the Kettering store since the war. The party of 33 included manager Francis Watts (in striped blazer), who became the town's "Mr Furniture". The grandson of the founder joined the Kettering firm in 1929, aged 17, and later became director and chairman. Francis served on the council for 12 years, becoming Mayor of Kettering in 1961/62. He was founder chairman of Kettering Round Table and in 1969, marking his 40th year in the town, he was made president of Kettering Chamber of Trade. When the Post Office buildings were being demolished to make way for the Newborough Centre in 1975, Francis doggedly remained the last trader in the block, only moving out under protest after threatened with legal action to evict him. The shop moved to smaller premises in Dalkeith Place (now the Earl of Dalkeith pub) and the Kettering business finally closed in 1985, beaten by the new trend for out-of-town superstores. Mr Watts, who kindly loaned these photographs, now lives in retirement in Weston Favell. (*Francis Watts*)

The "Co-op"

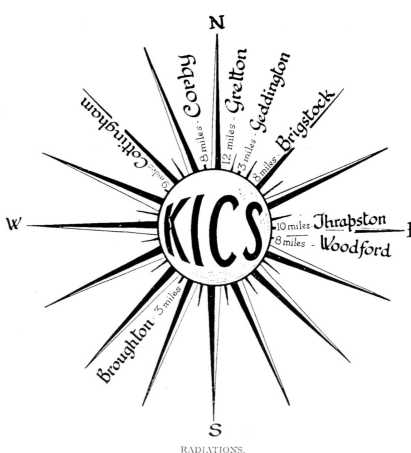

RADIATIONS.
From the Kettering Industrial Co-operative Society Limited.

The No.1 store of Kettering Industrial Co-operative Society on Bakehouse Hill, transferred from High Street in 1871, five years after the movement was formed in the town to give help to the poor. Thousands of Kettering people were employed by the Co-op's shops, depots and factories, and members shopping at its stores would receive a "dividend" on their purchases. When KICS celebrated its Diamond Jubilee in 1926, it boasted 13 grocery branches, 10 butcher's shops and various other departments in Kettering alone. In addition there were eight grocery and three butchery stores in the neighbouring villages of Corby, Broughton, Woodford, Geddington, Brigstock, Cottingham and Thrapston. At one time the Co-op had its own bakery, bank, corn shop, cabinet works, hairdressers, confectioners, drapery, dairy, piggery and poultry farm, not to mention huge shoe and clothing factories. Its Central Stores and Arcade, a vast complex fronting both Montagu Street and Newland Street, opened in 1930 and its multi-purpose Central Hall became a popular venue for stage shows, dinners, dances, plays, concerts, wedding receptions and business meetings. The Bakehouse Hill store was rebuilt with offices in 1894 and demolished for the new Gold Street development in the 1960s. (*Tony Smith*)

A postcard of Montagu Street in the 1960s showing Montagu House, the vast headquarters and showpiece shopping emporium of the KICS. Alterations and extensions carried out in 1930 had transformed the three-storey premises into a modern London-style department store with main entrances in Newland Street and Montagu Street, linked by an attractive arcade with window displays, chairs for tired shoppers and even cycle stands. Old stables and an ugly yard made way for the new Central Stores, which boasted furniture, drapery, men's outfitting and new boot departments. The first floor had special sections for millinery, baby linen and children's clothes, and other features included a tea room, rest room and roof garden for summer teas! In later years furniture and bedding departments were based on upper floors. (*Robert Wharton*)

The old KICS food store remained empty in the early 1980s after the merger with the Leicestershire Co-op, whose plans to build a new superstore in Northfield Avenue were initially turned down by Kettering Council. But the Co-op won its appeal in 1983 and two years later the £6 million complex opened, creating more than 200 jobs. As well as a supermarket, the site included a restaurant, petrol station, toy shop and garden centre (the store has since added electrical, furniture, cookware, clothing, stationery and music/video departments). Argos took over the former food store in 1987 and Berry Bros took over the 13,000 sq ft corner section at Newland Street/Montagu Street. (*Evening Telegraph*)

The chapter on transport in my previous book, *The Kettering Album*, closed with a 1910 picture of a Foden steam lorry used by Kettering furniture removers W. A. Pink (later Pink and Jones). This picture from the 1930s shows a motor van belonging to the Ford Street firm outside Linnett's newsagents in Sheep Street where a delicate piano moving operation is taking place. The company's history goes back more than a century to 1885, when Mr Pink arrived in Kettering from his native Yorkshire with a donkey and cart. Within four years his small coal business branched out into furniture removal, and he ran the firm almost single-handedly until adding Darlington man John Jones to his two-man staff in 1933. Eleven years later the pair became partners and the rest, as they say, is history.

Although Mr Pink died in 1953, aged 90, the firm retained the name and, after being taken over by Harrison and Rowley of Bedford in 1996, it became known as Britannia Pink and Jones, based in Baron Avenue off Telford Way (they even helped the *ET* move to Ise Park last year). Linnetts was a well-known Kettering concern and its Sheep Street premises, squeezed between the Cherry Tree and New Inn (later Market Tavern), had been in the family since 1910. When Jean Linnett retired in 1988 after running the shop for 20 years, the *Evening Telegraph* presented her with flowers as a thank-you for selling its papers. The shop, set up by her late husband's father Joseph, was taken over by Dalbir Mann and family, and to this day is still known to locals as Linnetts. (*Britannia Pink and Jones*)

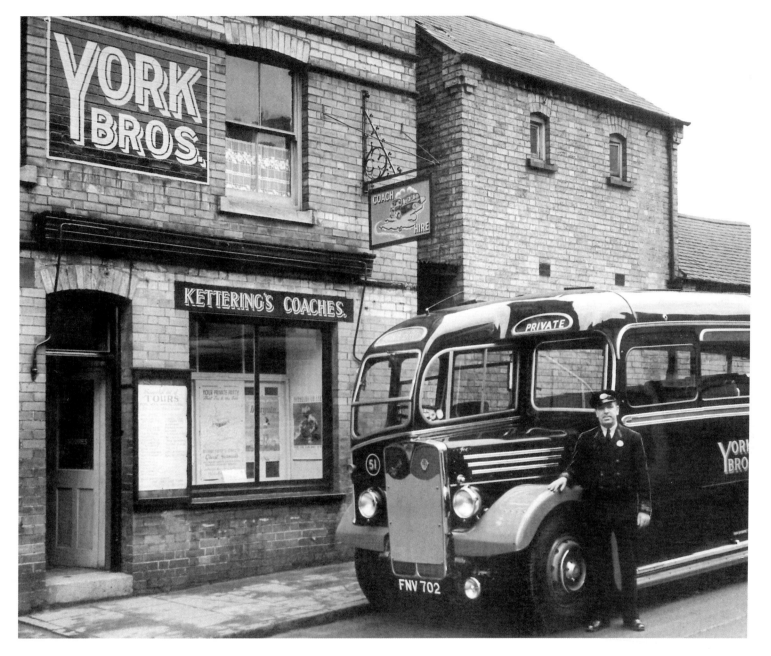

The old Market Street booking office of Cogenhoe coach firm York Bros, opened in the 1950s as the forerunner to the company's current chain of 17 travel agents in and around the county. Parked outside is *HMS Ocean*, one of Yorks' "fleet" of coaches with such seafaring names as *HMS Illustrious*, *HMS Kenya*, *HMS Ark Royal* and even *HMS King George V*. Founded in 1924, York Bros were among the pioneers of luxury coach travel in Britain. Their office at 13 Market Street (later moving to Newland Street) was run by Mr Reuben Henman, who had been a driver for the company since 1928. For a short time they also had a small depot in London Road, Kettering before taking over Bagshaws' former garage and workshop in Tanners Lane in 1955. I can remember Yorks providing the transport for primary school trips to London Airport and Wembley Stadium (for schoolboy internationals) during the early 1960s. (*Bob York*)

Alf Bailey's family music shop in Gold Street, pictured shortly before it closed in January 1985. The founder, who lived at Haydn House in Garfield Street, was a professor of music and well-known piano teacher with a remarkable record of no exam failures by his students for more than 20 years. He tuned, repaired and sold pianos for a living from 1889 and conducted his own orchestra, which performed at Christmas parties, winter balls, summer fêtes and bazaars. He was one of the lessees of the old Victoria Hall in Gold Street (later the Odeon cinema) and his company was responsible for booking entertainment when it became a professional theatre in 1907. The compact Gold Street shop opened just after World War I, selling musical instruments, sheet music and, later, gramophone records. Being a fan of so-called "progressive" rock music in the early 1970s, I often ordered LPs by rather obscure bands from the then proprietor Graham Bailey, grandson of Alf, and to his credit he had always heard of them and was able to oblige. (*Tony Smith*)

One of Kettering's oldest surviving businesses is Phillips, the drapers, which opened its Newland Street premises in 1887 and, rather remarkably, still trades there more than a century later. It was originally a branch of the well-known Northampton firm of Manchester Warehousemen, occupying rather tiny premises on the ground floor of No. 3 Newland Street, but soon took over No. 5 and the two upper storeys, previously the offices of the old Waterworks Company. At the turn of the century, when this picture was taken, the firm boasted it had the largest stock of dresses and furnishing in Kettering. Its spacious showrooms displayed a wide variety of goods, from dress materials, linens, furs and flannels to curtains and carpets, blankets, bedsteads and bedding. (*Tony Smith*)

Cold meat specialist Ernest Lewin opened his first shop in Newland Street (now the Button Boutique) on 5 October 1922 and this photograph of it was taken during the same decade, with manager Sid Bowd (right) and an assistant pictured outside. The shop later moved to High Street (later Sketchleys) with Ernest's son Ted taking over the business, and at one time the family firm also had premises in Montagu Street and a Corby branch. When Ted died in 1993, aged 84, the shop (in its present location on the corner of High Street and Crispin Place) closed on the afternoon of the funeral as a mark of respect. Ted, succeeded by his son Bill, was founder member of Kettering Probus Club and a member of the town's bowling and cricket clubs. Lewins, now more of a delicatessen, moved into its current premises in 1961. It was formerly The Grotto sweet shop and tea rooms, a picture of which appears in my previous book, *The Kettering Album*. (*Bill Lewin*)

"The Puzzle"

This higgledy-piggledy building (left) in Horsemarket, pictured shortly before its demolition in April 1952, was built in the mid-nineteenth century and known affectionately by local people as "The Puzzle". In its lifetime it had housed a gown shop, sewing machine shop, paint shop and a family butcher's shop (see picture above of W. S. Shrive and Son, circa 1913), with its upper floor at one time used for flats. But in its final years, the brickwork was cracked, walls leaned over, ceilings sagged and the wooden lintels had rotted away. Because of the danger it posed, workmen dismantled the building tile by tile, brick by brick and rafter by rafter.

The site – to the left of the former Cross Keys Restaurant (now O'Malleys) as shown in the smaller picture – was later incorporated into the town's development plan to become a small garden and bus shelter, and is now the repositioned taxi rank.
(*Kettering Leader and Guardian and inset, Leslie Breed*)

At the turn of the century the corner premises of "The Puzzle" were occupied by Charles Bailey, men's tailor, hatter, shirt-maker and hosier. Mr Bailey took over the three-storey building (then known as Dalkeith Arcade) in 1889 and soon established a reputation for quality clothing and excellent personal service. Two years after he opened the shop, the British Industrial Publishing Company described the young proprietor as "a thorough master of his trade, who devotes personal attention to the execution of all orders, hence the work is invariably well performed and always to the entire satisfaction of his patrons."
(*Tony Smith*)

6. Leisure

The Odeon cinema in Gold Street was officially opened on 19 September 1936 by Mr Stephen Shillizzi of Loddington Hall. An invited audience saw the Eddie Cantor film *Strike Me Pink* as the main feature, plus Universal News and the cartoon *Robber Kitten*. The former Victoria Picture House could seat 1,090 – 740 in the stalls and 350 in the circle. Daily shows were continuous from 2pm, with three performances on Saturday, at prices from 6d to 1s.6d. The Odeon was not licensed for Sunday screening until 1947, although there were special openings for troops on leave during the war. A "world premiere" of the film *The Browning Version*, starring Jean Kent and Nigel Patrick, was held there in March 1952, with 17-year-old cast member Brian Smith making a personal appearance and addressing the audience. In its heyday, Saturday night queues for the Odeon often stretched down Gold Street beyond the old Grammar School building. The Rank Organisation closed the cinema on 29 October 1960, the last picture show being the Norman Wisdom comedy *There Was a Crooked Man*. It re-opened as a bingo hall on 8 November 1961, closed again in 1972 and was demolished two years later. (*Kettering Leader and Guardian*)

"The Pav"

The old Gaumont Pavilion in High Street, known affectionately as "The Pav", replaced the Electric Pavilion in 1927, introducing the first "talkies" in town in 1929. The Gaumont-British Picture Corporation, to give its full name, was the third owner since the picture house opened in 1913. Gaumont became part of the J. Arthur Rank Organisation in 1942 and is pictured here in 1958, five years after a young actress called Joan Collins officially re-opened the building after major renovations. The cinema, like Miss Collins, had an impressive frontage (sorry!), its marble-stepped entrance lit up by 48 electric lights. It closed on 10 October 1959 and was demolished the following year, to be replaced by the new Boots store. (*Tony Smith*)

The Empire

The Empire cinema in Eskdaill Street, unkindly dubbed the "fleapit" or "bughutch", opened on Monday, 3 May 1920. It was the second purpose-built picture house in town (after "The Pav") and also the smallest, seating just 400 downstairs and 100 in the small balcony, including a number of double seats which proved popular with courting couples. A bijou orchestra provided music until the first "talkies" were shown from 1931. Films were booked at Mr Bamford's photographic shop in Montagu Street. He was one of three partners, with Jack Sherwood, owner of the Coliseum, later assuming some control. It became the New Empire in the 1940s but closed on 19 June 1954. The building became a warehouse for A. R. & W. Cleaver opposite in December 1955, but since May 1989 it has been occupied by the Selecta Tyre and Exhaust Centre. (*Kettering Leader and Guardian*)

The Granada, which replaced the Regal cinema in January 1948, is best remembered by many for its stage shows and concerts during the 1950s and 60s. Stars who trod its boards included such comedy legends as Flanagan and Allen and Morecambe and Wise, top bandleaders Joe Loss, Jack Hylton and Henry Hall, and former "Forces' Sweetheart" Vera Lynn. Popular sixties package tours brought Kettering music fans their first glimpse of such pop idols as Billy Fury, The Who and Dusty Springfield – everyone from Joe Brown and his Bruvvers to Lulu and her Luvvers! Rock 'n' roll rebel Gene Vincent made his entrance astride a motorbike and the Rolling Stones, supported by Marty Wilde and the Ronettes in 1964, were described by *ET* critic Alex Gordon as "refugees from a barber's shop". My dad paid 7s.6d. (37p) for me to see The Searchers, Gerry and the Pacemakers, Brian Poole and the Tremeloes, and Dave Berry and the Cruisers (billtoppers Freddie and the Dreamers were pelted with jelly babies by screaming teenage girls!). In the 1970s there were memorable Granada concerts by Roy Wood's Wizzard (which I reviewed for the *ET*), the Bay City Rollers and Little Richard before the theatre became a bingo hall in 1974. Happy days! (*Evening Telegraph*)

SAVOY, KETTERING

General Manager (For REGINALD SALBERG)
and Licensee .... REYNOR HEALY
Telephone No.—2794.

1947 REPERTORY SEASON
Nightly at 7.15 — Saturdays at 6.0 & 8.30
Matinee Thursday at 2.30
Theatre Box-Office Open Daily
10.0 to 8.15

Seats may be booked from usual agencies or by telephone. Permanent and Telephone Bookings must be claimed 15 minutes before the rise of the curtain.

:: Programme Notes ::
"MARY ROSE" our choice for next week needs no introduction to our patrons. This charming ever-green classic by Sir J. M. Barrie continues to enchant all who love the theatre. The very name—"MARY ROSE" ideally epitomises the wistful, haunting beauty of the play.
We regret that Miss MARY JORDAN will be leaving us at the end of this week to fulfill an engagement to play the leading part in Mr. Barry O'Brien's tour of "Man About The House."

:: Forthcoming Attractions ::
REPERTORY SEASON 1947
24th November "PRIVATE LIVES"
By NOEL COWARD
1st December "NIGHT MUST FALL"
By EMLYN WILLIAMS
8th December "YES AND NO" By KENNETH HORNE (another comedy from the author of "Fools Rush In.")
:: Xmas Season ::
26th Dec. until "LILAC TIME"
3rd Jan. 1948
5th Jan. for 1 week "JOEL'S CIRCUS"
12th Jan. for 2 weeks "RED RIDING HOOD"
26th Jan. for 1 week "CINDERELLA"
Box Office opening for above Xmas attractions on 24th November.   Book in Advance.
Usual Booking Agencies :
KETTERING   Alf. Bailey
CORBY   Frames
WELLINGBOROUGH   Iresons.
RUSHDEN   Nevilles.
:: Sunday Film Programme ::
"WINGED VICTORY" (U)   5-30 and 7-53
Lon McAllister, Jeanne Crain, Edmund O'Brien
"HOT WATER" (U) and "IN HOLIDAY MOOD" (U)

PROGRAMME

WEEK COMMENCING MONDAY, NOV. 10th, 1947

THE REGINALD SALBERG REPERTORY COMPANY in

TONS OF MONEY

By WILL EVANS and VALENTINE

Characters in order of their appearance :—

Sprules (*a Butler*)	PETER ASHBY
Miss Benita Mullett	HILARY VERNON
Louise Allington	NORAH WILLIAMS
Aubrey Henry Maitland Allington	GEOFFREY LUMSDEN
Giles (*a Gardener*)	NORMAN ATKYNS
James Chesterman (*a Solicitor*)	TIM HUDSON
Jean Everard	MARY JORDAN
Henery	CHARLES MARDEL
George Maitland	JOHN SPICER

The Play produced by JOHN MAXWELL
The Set designed and painted by
JOHN LEWIS

Stage Manager ...... NORMAN ATKYNS
Assisted by : MAUREEN REEVE, JOHN SPICER
and DESMOND HASKELL

ACT ONE

Aubrey Henry Maitland Allington's house at Marlow.

(*Three weeks elapse between Acts I and III*).

ACT TWO

The Same   (Afternoon)

(*One day elapses between Acts II and III*).

ACT THREE

The Same   (Late Afternoon)

Furniture kindly supplied by F. A. Watts & Co., and by Phillips's Warehouse Ltd. China etc., by Day's China & Glass Showrooms. Electrical fittings by The Farringdon Electric Supply and the Borough of Kettering Electricity Dept. Furs by M. Blain & Son. Flowers by The Farm Shop and K.I.C.S., Windmill Avenue Nurseries. Antiques by W. G. Keach and C. W. Ward. Carpets by Ernest Woodcock Ltd. Silverware by A. A. Thornton.   Cigarettes by Abdulla

The Savoy in Russell Street was popular both as a cinema and theatre. It was officially opened on Saturday, 21 May 1938 by Cllr Walter Dyson, last chairman of the old Kettering Urban District Council. It rose from the ashes of the former Coliseum, destroyed by a furious fire on 6 April 1937. The "Col", like its predecessor the Avenue Theatre, attracted many stars of variety, including Gracie Fields, Harry Tate and Lily Langtry. This tradition was continued by the Savoy in the 1940s and 1950s with appearances by the likes of Tommy Trinder, Arthur Askey, Sandy Powell, Will Fyfe, George Robey and Ted Ray. It was also a popular venue for touring repertory companies and from 1948 to 1951 the Northampton "Rep" leased the theatre and presented weekly plays. The bingo boom of the 1960s robbed the Savoy of its ground floor, the upstairs being converted to two studio cinemas. It finally became the Ohio cinema before its inevitable demise in 1997 just a few months before the opening of the new eight-screen Odeon complex in Pegasus Court. There are plans to demolish the Russell Street building to make way for flats.

A production shot of the cast of *Floradora*, performed by Kettering Operatic Society at the Central Hall from 5 to 9 April 1949. In 1997 the society celebrated its Golden Jubilee with two special gala shows at the McKinlay Theatre. It was initially formed by members of local youth groups to give post-war teenagers a creative outlet. The first show, *Paris in Spring*, funded by 30 town businesses and other patrons, was a huge success. In its early years the driving force behind the society was the late and legendary Miss Gladys Riseley, the enthusiastic music teacher at Park Junior School, who directed the first six shows. In the society's heyday of the 1950s and '60s such classic musicals as *Oklahoma*, *Showboat*, *The Desert Song*, *Annie Get Your Gun*, *Carousel* and *The Merry Widow* were staged, as well as annual pantomimes. From 1955 to 1967 the group switched venues from the Central Hall to the Savoy, but returned to the Central Hall until it closed in 1975. Much of its success in recent years has been down to its vastly experienced producer Ray Jeffery. The male actors pictured here in 1947 are (from left) Ted Southwell, John Williams, Horace Simpson, Bob Sallabanks and Jack Stanbury. The ladies are Janet Toseland, Sheila Humphrey, Doreen Chapman and Doreen Perry.

(*Mary Green*)

During the swinging sixties The Tin Hat in Britannia Road, Kettering was acknowledged as one of the top rock and blues venues in the country. This ramshackle club – long since demolished – booked a host of top rock bands for regular Saturday night "gigs", including such music legends as Jethro Tull, Fleetwood Mac, Cream (featuring Eric Clapton) and The Four Tops. Other well-known names who appeared there were The Foundations, P P Arnold, Rory Gallagher's Taste, Family, The Nice and John Mayall's Bluesbreakers. Hordes of youngsters would arrive by car and coach from miles around – Rushden, Wellingborough, Corby, Bedford, even London and Birmingham. Inevitably there were complaints from local residents in Britannia Road, Rockingham Road and Northfield Avenue when hundreds of teenagers would (allegedly) run riot after spilling out of the club at the end of the evening, singing, shouting and revving their motor cycles ("Midnight Madness" said the *Kettering Leader*). The Tin Hat, sited behind the Poppies football ground, was also used as a fans' social club on match days. I can remember, when just a young boy, my late father taking me there at half-time for a bottle of pop and bag of crisps! (*Kettering Leader*)

The Old White Horse Hotel in High Street was a popular town centre "watering hole" during the first half of the century (and a favoured haunt of journalists from the *ET* offices behind, so I'm told). The original Old White Horse, demolished in 1905, was sited to the left of this building where the Gas Board offices are in the picture. Its replacement, with its distinctive domed spire, was erected on the corner of Huxloe Place. The Old White Horse (not to be confused with the New White Horse Inn), owned for many years by Phipps brewery in Northampton, closed on Tuesday, 24 November 1959 when its future was uncertain and negotiations for its sale had fallen through. Farewell gifts were presented by regular customers to the last landlord Ron Thornton before he called "Time" for the last time. The premises are now occupied by Burton Menswear (formerly Montagu Burton), which opened on 23 February 1962. As a special offer, free suits were given away to the first six old-age pensioners through its doors. (*Kettering Leader*)

The elegant entrance to Kettering's much-missed Central Hall, the grand and spacious multi-purpose theatre complex opened by the town's Co-op in Montagu Street in October 1929. For almost half a century the impressive auditorium, complete with balcony and gallery, became the town's top venue for stage shows, concerts, plays, dinners, dances and wedding receptions (it even hosted the World Snooker Final in 1934). The building's Art Deco style included a high vaulted roof, decorative glass ceiling panels and splendid marble steps, as pictured here. Inside it boasted 850 seats (600 downstairs), a maple dance floor and a kitchen capable of catering for 600 people. Amazingly, the hall was mothballed in the mid-1970s and used as a warehouse, and promising plans to revive the hall have so far failed to materialise. (*Tony Smith*)

The Peacock Inn

The old Peacock Inn in Lower Street pictured in November 1959 when it was closed, waiting to be demolished and rebuilt as a more modern alehouse. The pub has occupied this site for more than 300 years and among the famous visitors it claimed was Charles Dickens, when he was staying at the White Hart (now the Royal Hotel). It also laid on a memorable six-course lunch in 1834 for members of the newly-formed Kettering Gas Company. When this picture was taken, the Peacock was said to be the oldest public house in Kettering, and it contained some fine oak panelling (also a feature of the new building), part of which was standing in Cromwell's day. Also demolished with the old pub were the house and shop next door, creating a new corner site. The new pub, restyled and refurnished by brewers Bass of Burton-on-Trent, had a saloon, smoke room, lounge bar and off-licence shop (its first landlord was Lionel Smart). The Peacock underwent another transformation in 1996 with a major £340,000 refit in a bid to attract more families and business people. A new £40,000 beer garden, seating up to 60 people and lit by Victorian-style lamps, opened on Easter Sunday, 1998. (*Kettering Leader and Guardian*)

This attractive corner at the 'dog leg' of Market Street has been occupied by a number of different shops in recent years, but for more than half of this century it was the premises of the Sun Hotel. Like the Crown Inn in Gold Street, it closed in June 1960 as part of Phipps' policy of reducing the number of town-centre pubs and releasing their sites for shops. How long a public house had been there is anyone's guess, but as Market Street is one of Kettering's oldest thoroughfares, there is no doubt the present fairly modern building replaced a much older hostelry in 1893. Originally known as the Sun Inn, it stood a little further along the street, and its last landlord was George Breakspear. Historically, the site is important as the birthplace in 1803 of the famous missionary William Knibb. In more recent times, during the early 1970s, I remember it as the Laramie Bar (later the Astoria, then El Caramba), a somewhat dingy late-night drinking club for customers spilling out of the Gaiety (formerly the Golden Lion, now Watercress Harry's) just across the road. When this was written, the site (from left) was occupied by the Get Ahead unisex hair salon (previously Santos' barbers), Brides' bridal wear shop, Annogen the jewellers and Jasmire Ltd, an adult training centre. This picture was taken in July 1960.

(Kettering Leader)

Once upon a time there were two rival public houses right next to each other in Rockingham Road. The group of people pictured here, whom I have been unable to identify but are presumably bar staff or customers, are standing outside the Hare and Hounds in the 1950s, and further behind them is the Vine. Examining the photograph more closely, it's interesting to reflect how relatively recent the advent of the motor car has been in so many lives of ordinary people. In those days bikes were parked outside pubs with no fear of theft, whilst beyond the van is a bus stop for those too far gone to pedal home. Both of these taverns were eventually demolished along with neighbouring buildings to become the new Electricity Board headquarters. Today, of course, it is the site of Sainsbury's superstore. (*Evening Telegraph*)

The Fleur de Lys

The former Fleur de Lys pub occupied a commanding position in Newland Street and became the latest victim of Phipps' controversial policy of fewer pubs and more houses. Together with the Vine and Hare and Hounds, the "Flue", as it was nicknamed, was a firm favourite of Kettering and Cransley furnacemen in the old days. Before World War I, when licensing hours were not regulated, these three pubs, being the nearest to the old furnaces, would open especially for shift workers leaving off just after 6am and dying for a pint. After closing in March 1960, the Fleur de Lys remained empty for more than a year before it was pulled down to make way for a new £25,000 block of shops. After negotiations with a supermarket fizzled out, the three shop units were eventually taken by Gerald S. White (whose Dalkeith Place business sold prams and baby clothes), Blanchflowers garage (based in Northampton Road) and Fabrics Interior of Leicester. Today the former pub site is occupied by Gerald S. White (now selling carpets and curtains), Colemans the stationers, and M. C. Edwards, insurance brokers, with Argos to the right. (*Tony Smith*)

Wicksteed Park

For almost 80 years Wicksteed Park has been one of the region's top attractions. Despite the introduction of more modern amusements in recent years, the leisure complex has retained much of its old-world charm and many of its original features. The old children's playground pictured here had changed very little over the years until replaced in 1988 by modern brightly-coloured and safer play equipment. This part of the park is still free of charge and is open all year round, remaining true to founder Charles Wicksteed's original dream. To this day "Wickies" is still run by the small charity trust set up by Mr Wicksteed in 1916, with all income from car park fees, refreshments and rides ploughed back into the park's upkeep and development. When I was at Kettering Grammar School in the late 1960s this playground was where many boys met pupils from the nearby High School (now Southfield) during the lunch break. (*Tony Smith*)

Wicksteed lake covered in a blanket of snow after the terrible blizzards in February 1963. The 30-acre boating lake was the park's main attraction in its early years, along with the wide open spaces. Preliminary digging and levelling work, including the clearing of a wooded plantation, began before World War I and was completed afterwards. Initially there were just a few rowing boats, compared with more than a hundred by the 1960s. During cold winters the water would freeze over and skaters would appear from nowhere, chancing their lives as they couldn't really know how thick the ice was. (*Frank Corvesor*)

Record crowds thronged Wicksteed Park on 8 August 1965 when an estimated 60,000 children and parents attended the annual meeting of the Tingha and Tucker Club. Tingha and Tucker were two puppet koala bears (catchphrase: "Woomerang, boomerang!") who had their own teatime show on Midlands TV. That day also saw the town's longest traffic jam, stretching at one point from the park, through Kettering and out on the A43 towards Broughton. The children's show was hosted by "Auntie" Jean Morton, pictured (*inset*) in 1970 at the club's eighth – and last – meeting. This time only a quarter of an expected 20,000 people descended on Wicksteeds, but they all had a great time. In a striking red and white dress, Auntie Jean and the famous bears boarded the miniature train for a trip halfway round the lake, and then transferred to the stage for a rapturous welcome from the eagerly awaiting children. Despite a sharp rain shower, the show went on with a number of special guests, including Willie Wombat and "Uncle" Pat Astley. In the second half, nine finalists took part in a song competition, auditions for which had been held in the ballroom that morning. Amongst the audience during the afternoon was a party from Manfield Orthopaedic Hospital, Northampton. The children there had made a boomerang, which they presented to Miss Morton. The event was later televised over two editions of the programme.
(*Evening Telegraph*)

If you were among dozens of children who had a splashing time at Wicksteed Park on 10 June 1960, then you might just spot yourself in this people-packed picture taken at the children's bathing pool (I was only five then, but was probably queuing up to have an even wetter time on the water chute). Almost every summer during the 1960s, attendance records in the park were being broken. In 1964 alone, park staff dealt with 80,000 cars and 4,000 coaches, gave half-a-million rides on the train and 120,000 rides on the roller coaster (opened in 1961). By the mid-1960s traffic snarl-ups in Barton Road, Pytchley Road and London Road were so bad that police liaised with the AA and the park to set up diversions on peak days to ease the bumper-to-bumper congestion. (*Kettering Leader*)

An action shot from an exciting Kettering Rowing Club regatta on Wicksteed Park lake in 1949. The group was formed shortly after the park opened in 1921, using primitive skiffs on the newly-built boating lake. Early regattas were novelty events for Kettering, attracting thousands of curious spectators, but it wasn't until the 1930s that serious racing began. At dusk, motorists would drive down to the water's edge to illuminate the lake with their headlamps, but only four-seater boats (no "eights") were allowed, as the third-of-a-mile course was the smallest in the country. At first the club used an old railway carriage as a boathouse until the park provided a proper building (pictured here), and when rowing stopped during World War II this was used to house evacuees. In 1927 members moved "upmarket" when they acquired a second-hand Rolls-Royce Phantom I (for £85!) to ferry boats and up to 14 people to events (pictured inset). The club's finest hour came when it reached the final of the Henley Regatta in 1955. Using a boat which members made themselves, they survived four heats before losing narrowly to a team from Thames. The last regatta was held in 1969 and the club folded in 1978, but 35 ex-members attended a reunion and buffet at the George Hotel on 23 September 1997. (*Graham Arber*)

Glorious weather greeted the informal opening of Mill Road Recreation Ground on the afternoon of Sunday, 22 May 1925. Large numbers of people flocked to the two-acre park to enjoy music by Kettering Town Band, under the leadership of Mr J. Woolley. Among the local councillors present were Harry Potter, Messrs J. Haynes, J. E. P. Dainty, J. R. Sadler, T. Barlow, C. Mayes and Charles Wicksteed. Town clerk John Bond and his assistant John Chaston also attended.

Originally wasteground, the park had been transformed by the council, thanks largely to a generous donation by Kettering boot and shoe manufacturer Frank Wright. Bordered by Mill Road, Carey Street and, on the east side, St Mary's School in Fuller Street (to be demolished and rebuilt 50 years later), the ground was mostly turfed and contained a small shrubbery, flower bed and a few trees. Under the classic headline "Another lung for Kettering" the *Evening Telegraph* report said: "The provision of the 'Rec' meets a great need in the eastern part of the town. It serves first and foremost as a splendid playground for children, who doubtless will make the best of it." (*Robert Wharton*)

The future of Kettering Recreation Centre in Northampton Road has been uncertain since its closure in 1993. The former Drill Hall dates back to 1936 and during World War II, when still run by the Army, hundreds of servicemen spent their last night in the county there before going to the front. National conscripts and Northants Yeomanry troops were based there before and after the war, armoured cars were inspected inside the building, and troops who trained there during wartime often slept in the hall on straw mattresses. For many years afterwards it was used by Territorials and the Signals Squadron before the Ministry of Defence sold it to Kettering Borough Council in 1969. For a while it was hired out to local organisations and sports groups, the main hall used for badminton, basketball, boxing, volleyball, fencing and keep fit classes (I played five-a-side football there many times). Kettering and District Horticultural Society and the Cage Bird Society even used it for annual shows. Clive Hall took over as manager in 1972 after an £8,000 scheme to officially turn it into a sports centre, and four years later roller skating was held there, which was initially hailed a big success. It was finally killed off by plans for the new Kettering Leisure Village, and closed on 23 July 1993 – the same day the £13 million centre opened off Northampton Road. Plans by the Bedford Pilgrims Housing Association to build ten three-bedded homes and a 12-bed care unit for blind and disabled children were put on hold in 1998 following a dispute over ownership of the land.

(*Tony Smith*)

7. People

Canon Frank Pearce and his wife Josie came to Kettering in 1970 when he was appointed Rector, a post he served with diligence and vigour until his retirement in 1994. As a former provincial journalist in his native Mansfield, Canon Pearce had a nose for a good news story and his often controversial views in the parish newsletter were guaranteed to make headlines in the *Evening Telegraph*. His contribution to town life included being chaplain to the town's Sea Cadets and Air Training Corps, a vice-president of the Civic Society, president of the HQ Division of St John Ambulance and chaplain of both Kettering General and St Mary's Hospitals. Josie, known to friends as just Jo, was the town's Superintendent Registrar until resigning in 1988 to devote herself to the office of Mayoress of Kettering. She later returned to her job and was also a magistrate, president of the Parkinson's Disease Society and former County Commissioner of Guides, her community efforts earning her the MBE in the Queen's birthday honours in 1998. The couple are pictured with daughter Rachel, five, and son Martin, two, on their arrival in Kettering in April 1970. Rachel went on to work in the *Evening Telegraph* advertising department, and Martin once ran the Samuel Pepys pub at Slipton.
(*Evening Telegraph*)

John Turner Stockburn (1825-1922)

John Turner Stockburn (left), who died in 1922 at the age of 96, pioneered many projects which transformed Kettering and prepared the town for progress in the twentieth century. The "Grand Old Man of Northamptonshire Liberalism" spent 50 years in local government and was the driving force behind the founding of Kettering General Hospital, the School Board, Kettering Water Company and the Local Board (both of which he chaired) and Kettering Liberal Club. When the Local Board became Kettering Urban Council in 1894, "JTS" remained chairman for four years, stepping down at the age of 73. Mr Stockburn lived at the Mission House for 64 years and for a while owned Chesham House opposite. As well as running a corset factory in Northall Street, he was deacon of Toller Chapel and one of the first two middle-class Nonconformists to be made magistrate (at Gladstone's insistence) He also served as county councillor and for many years chaired Kettering Gas Company and Northamptonshire Printing and Publishing Company, owners of the *Evening Telegraph*.

Ernest Timson (1902-1987)

Kettering industrialist and town councillor Ernest Timson (right) was chairman and managing director of Timson's, the printing machinery firm founded by his father Arthur in 1896 and still thriving. The former Kettering Grammar School pupil was awarded the MBE in 1949 for his work as chairman of the county committee of the Regional Board for Industry (an OBE followed in 1960). Ernest, who died in 1987 aged 85, served on Kettering Council for 16 years, chaired the Kettering Social Welfare League for many years, and was the first chairman of Kettering Youth Committee. He was also vice president of both Kettering and County Cricket Clubs, a deacon at Fuller Baptist Church and a member of the Council of the Baptist Union of Great Britain and Ireland.

Some of Kettering's luminaries are pictured on the platform during Speech Day at Kettering Grammar School on 11 November 1921. At that time the school had around 250 boys and staff consisted of ten masters and two mistresses. The headmaster was John Irwin Scott, noted as a disciplinarian, who took over the post in 1913 and died in 1943, just a year after retiring through ill health. He was also first president of the Old Cytringanians, the "old boys" association which continues today. This picture was taken in the hall of the school in Bowling Green Road (later to become the borough council chamber). Pictured from left are: Miss Dorr (governor), Mrs Scott (wife of headmaster), Mr S. J. Lloyd (chairman of the county education committee), Mr H. G. Gotch (chairman of the school governors), Mr J. I. Scott (headmaster), Miss Hilda Wicksteed (governor), Mr J. L. Holland (county director of education), Cllr John Loake (governor) and Mr F. J. Thorpe (principal of Wellingborough Technical School). After the presentation of prizes to pupils, the Speech Day closed with songs from the school choir, with Mr A. H. Essam on the piano. (*Tony Smith*)

William Timpson (1849-1929)

Rothwell-born William Timpson (left), pioneer of the local boot and shoe industry, has been described as Kettering's greatest businessman. His first premises was a hut in the garden of a house in Station Road in 1879, later taking over an old weaving factory in Market Street. But it was from his ultra-modern Bath Road factory, producing 20,000 pairs of shoes from the 1920s onwards, that he built his empire of 262 shops and 210 repairing outlets. His home was Sunnylands, the Jacobean-style mansion in Headlands (designed by J. A. Gotch and now St Peter's School), with much of his social life devoted to Fuller Church, where a memorial tablet to him was unveiled in 1935. He was a deacon, beloved Sunday School teacher and Bible Class leader, chairman of Kettering Liberal Association and a member of the Local Board, but deafness cut short his political career.

Frank Hutchen (1870-1942)

For four decades, former printer's lad Frank Hutchen (right) guided the destiny of the *Evening Telegraph*, establishing the paper as an organ of integrity in the community it served. He succeeded the *ET*'s first editor, Thomas Collings, in 1901 and was still working at his Dryland Street desk when he suffered a stroke and died two weeks short of his 72nd birthday. Mr Hutchen was a staunch Liberal, never smoked, drank or ate meat, and was an outspoken champion of the Temperance movement in Kettering. He steered the *ET* through its often difficult formative years and World War I, introducing many new machines, all of which he could operate himself. During World War II he launched the *ET*'s first major campaign, which raised £35,000 to buy seven Spitfires. Sadly he did not live to see the victory they helped accomplish. A keen sportsman, Frank helped found the Kettering and District Cricket League and the Kettering Football Combination. He was also a local historian, often giving lantern shows on old Kettering.

John Profumo

A picture of "Chrissie the Criss-Cross Girl" and her inventor John Profumo outside the *Evening Telegraph* offices in Dryland Street in July 1948. Mr Profumo became best known as the British Cabinet Minister whose affair with ex-showgirl and model Christine Keeler brought down Macmillan's government in 1963. But his political career began as Conservative MP for Kettering during World War II. The dashing young air pilot was a Second Lieutenant in the 1st Northamptonshire Yeomanry when his by-election victory in March 1940 made him, at 25, the youngest member of the House of Commons. During the war, Profumo was air staff officer at Field Marshall Alexander's headquarters in Italy.

After losing his seat in the landslide General Election of 1945, he remained Kettering's prospective Tory candidate until 1948, served as MP at Stratford for 13 years, and rose through the ranks of the Transport Ministry and Foreign Office before becoming Minister of War in 1960. Married to actress Valerie Hobson, Profumo was tipped as a future Prime Minister before the scandal.

Three-ply "Chrissie" (back to the above picture) was part of a road safety campaign in Kettering, the idea being to place her at zebra crossings to warn drivers who may have missed the Belisha beacons.
(*Kettering Leader and Guardian*)

NORTHAMPTONSHIRE   4th EDN.

Evening Telegraph

Oct. 4, 1897,   MONDAY FEBRUARY 1 1943   Price Three Halfpence

Ted Sismore

KETTERING MAN WAS OVER BERLIN AT ELEVEN A.M.

Dropped First Bomb That "Blew · Goering Off The Air"

A 21-YEAR-OLD Kettering clerk, who, up to the outbreak of war was engaged in the Treasurer's Department of Kettering Town Council, Pilot Officer Edward Barnes Sismore, had the thrill of dropping the first bomb on Berlin in the daylight raids on the German capital on Saturday, when the Nazi celebrations were thrown out of gear and Goering went to earth.

He is the only son of Mr. and Mrs. Claude Sismore, of 173, Neale-avenue, Kettering, who are very proud of his exploit. Mr Sismore, senior, is a cutter at the Kettering Clothing Co-operative Society Ltd.

The leader of the first airmen ever to bomb Berlin in daylight was Squadron Leader Reginald W. Reynolds, D.F.C., who is 24 years of age, and comes from Cheltenham. Many of the men who accompanied him were even younger

Stormy Trip

EIGI
PU

General Mov F

Slowly but re ing on, and the major engagem Army, writes R. tary commentat

The recent atta Germans in South are possibly design object of securing possible Rommel communications i northern Tunisian the Mareth Line. T

Ted Sismore, a former clerk of Kettering Council's treasury department, became a famous flying ace and the town's most decorated war hero. Pilot Officer Sismore, whose parents lived in Neale Avenue, was awarded the Distinguished Flying Cross for his part in the first daylight bombing raid over Berlin on 30 January 1943. He was a 21-year-old navigator in the first of three Mosquitos which bombed the radio station where Hermann Goering was to address the German nation, sending the humiliated Luftwaffe Commander scuttling to the nearest shelter. Ted went on to win the Distinguished Service Order for a daring daylight raid on the Zeiss lens works in 1943, later gaining two bars to his DFC. Promoted to Squadron Leader after the war, he made worldwide headlines with a record-breaking flight from London to Cape Town in a Mosquito in May 1947. Ted, who retired as an Air Commodore in 1976, now lives near Maldon, Essex. Another Kettering war hero, Len Sumpter, received the DFC and the Distinguished Flying Medal as one of the famous Dambuster pilots. Len, who died in 1993, aged 82, was born at the former Trades Club in Mill Road, where his father was a steward. (*Ted Sismore*)

REGAL
SUPER CINEMA
KETTERING
TO-DAY VE-DAY.

OPEN AS USUAL with
Grand Double Feature
Programme and
SPECIAL VICTORY NEWS REEL.

The King's Message will be Relayed
in The Theatre and Foyer.

OPEN WEDNESDAY,
12 noon to 11 p.m.

We maintain the wartime theme with this photograph of a group of Kettering people all set for a feast to celebrate VE Day in May 1945. They were all residents from the Edmund Street area ready to tuck in to tea at the Windmill Club. Front left is Mrs Zilph Petts, who ran the Edmund Street shop for many years, next to Miss Wulshire and Chick Petts. On the right are Jessie Bradshaw and teacher Mr Carter and his wife. Along with the rest of Britain, the end of the war in Europe was marked by similar street parties, both indoors and outdoors, throughout Kettering. Compared to neighbouring towns Rushden and Wellingborough, Kettering got off lightly as far as bomb damage was concerned, but many local men died fighting for their country. The town also became a home-from-home for American servicemen based at nearby Grafton Underwood. The "friendly invasion" of young Yanks, who often spent their Liberty Runs in the town's pubs and dance halls, led to many lifelong friendships (not to mention more than 150 GI brides!) Men serving at Grafton were even treated to English ice cream when the 384th Group bought manufacturing equipment from Wicksteed Park, which had been forced to stop production when rationing began. (*Tony Smith*)

Miss Gladys Riseley (1907-1984)

Gladys Riseley – Kettering's "Miss Music" – was a tremendous influence on the town's musical, educational and civic life. She taught for 40 years at Park (Road) Junior School, where she retired as deputy head in 1970. She was a councillor for ten years and secretary of the Duke of Edinburgh Award's Kettering committee. But her real passion was music: in her youth she was a singer and dancer, performing in an operetta at Rockingham Road Baptist Church at the age of eight. She was also founder, musical director and, later, president of Kettering Operatic Society and organiser of the town's annual Eisteddfod. To get the best out of her pupils, she could be quite formidable. I recall, as a child, being chastened by her during rehearsals for a combined schools production of Benjamin Britten's *Noye's Flude*. Ten years later, as a cub reporter, I received that same withering look after noisily entering the hall where Eisteddfod classes were being judged! Bizarrely, she once told me she was a big Harlem Globetrotters fan and her constant companion was her toy poodle Sixpence (pictured), bought for her by the cast of the show *Half A Sixpence* in 1970. She was presented with the MBE (by Prince Phillip) in 1964 and died in 1984, aged 76.

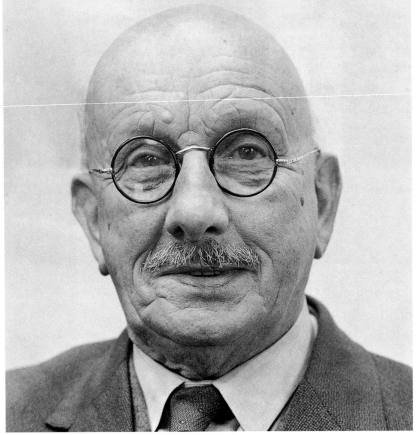

Alderman Dyson (1881-1968)

Alderman Walter Dyson, Mayor in 1949/50 and the first Freeman of the Borough in 1956, was the "father" of Kettering Council with an unequalled record of public service. After 16 years on Kettering Urban Council, he served on the new Borough Council since it was formed in 1938, and was a county councillor from 1946 to 1954. He worked at Kaycee Clothing for 40 years and was captain of the Co-op fire brigade for the same period. He was a member of St John Ambulance for an amazing 64 years, exactly half of that time as Kettering Corps Superintendent. A ward was named after him at St Crispin Hospital, Duston to honour his 17 years' service on the county mental health committee. He was also a keen trombonist and conducted the factory orchestra. I only met him once – when he presented me with a national art competition prize at Grange Primary School!

Kettering people from all walks of life attended a memorial service at Kettering Parish Church to pay their last tributes to King George VI. Hundreds of mourners, young and old, came from factories and shops, from the fields and the streets for the afternoon service on Friday, 5 February 1952. Half an hour before it was due to begin, several hundred were already praying privately in the church when a siren signalled two minutes silence at 2pm, the starting time of the King's funeral at Westminster. The silence was also observed in local shops, offices, factories, schools and homes – even bus drivers halted on their routes. Town cinemas and pubs did not open until 6pm and although shops stayed open they gave time off for any staff wishing to attend the service. The civic procession, led by the Munn and Felton Works Band wearing white mourning armlets, marched from the council offices in High Street. At the west door of the church they were met by the Archdeacon of Oakham, robed clergy and the combined choirs of the four Anglican churches in the town. Veterans of the Boer War and World War I, their medals proudly displayed, joined members of the British Legion and many other Kettering organisations represented at the service. The civic procession is seen here arriving at the church, headed by Inspector Davidge and Mace-bearer Price. Behind the Mayor and Mayoress, Ald. and Mrs Charles Goode, are Cllr C. Mayes, Cllr A. E. Munn, town clerk Mr Dunsford Price, Cllr A. E. Woodcock, Cllr Mrs.Stebbings and Ald. Mrs Frances Clarke, Ald. Walter Dyson and Ald. R Tailby. Kettering streets were deserted as residents listened to the radio or watched television coverage. In the evening Kettering and District Free Church Council held its own memorial service at Fuller Baptist Church. (*Judy Eden*)

Harry Potter (1876-1963)

Many Kettering people will know the name Harry Potter from the old people's flats named after him in London Road. But older readers knew him for his long and devoted service as a borough and county councillor. Mr Potter, who was born in Leicester but moved to Kettering in 1911, clocked up a remarkable 45 years' service on Kettering Council, including 25 years as finance committee chairman. His local government career ended after the elections of May 1963. Following three recounts, he was still tying with Ald. Mrs Frances Clarke and, being a gentleman, decided to withdraw.

Alderman Mrs Frances Clarke (1882-1966)

Alderman Mrs Frances Clarke, who joined Kettering Urban Council in 1931, became its first and only lady chairman in 1936 and was substitute Charter Mayor when Kettering became a borough in 1938. She was also the first lady chairman of Kettering Education Committe and was largely responsible for getting the Ronald Tree Nursery School in Laburnum Crescent off the ground in 1934 – the first such school in the county. Mrs Clarke was also former secretary and chairman of the town's Maternity and Child Welfare Committee. She and Cllr Potter (see above) were to have been invested together as Kettering's second and third Freemen of the Borough in 1964 but, sadly, Mr Potter died before the official ceremony.

Winning smiles from Kettering's Munn and Felton Works Band after another national triumph before a capacity audience of 8,000 at the Royal Albert Hall on 15 October 1960. The band scooped the first of six British Brass Band Championship titles at Crystal Palace in 1935, just two years after being formed at the factory by managing director Fred Felton. Its name was changed to the GUS (Footwear) Band in 1962 when the Great Universal Stores group bought out the firm, which employed 1,000 people at four Kettering factories. Under the baton of musical director Stanley Boddington (inset), GUS had a bulging trophy cabinet over the next decade, culminating in its World Championship victory in 1971.

The band recorded 30 albums, featured in many radio and TV broadcasts, and toured Europe and America. Mr Boddington, who died in 1986, aged 81, retired in 1975 – two years after a testimonial concert to mark his 40 years with the band. Under his successor Dr Keith Wilkinson, GUS won the BBC Best of Brass Competition in 1980 and 1981 and was BBC Band of the Year in 1983. The Desborough-based Rigid Containers Group replaced GUS as the band's sponsors in 1987, and a year later it won the British Open for the first time in 30 years. (*London Press Photos*)

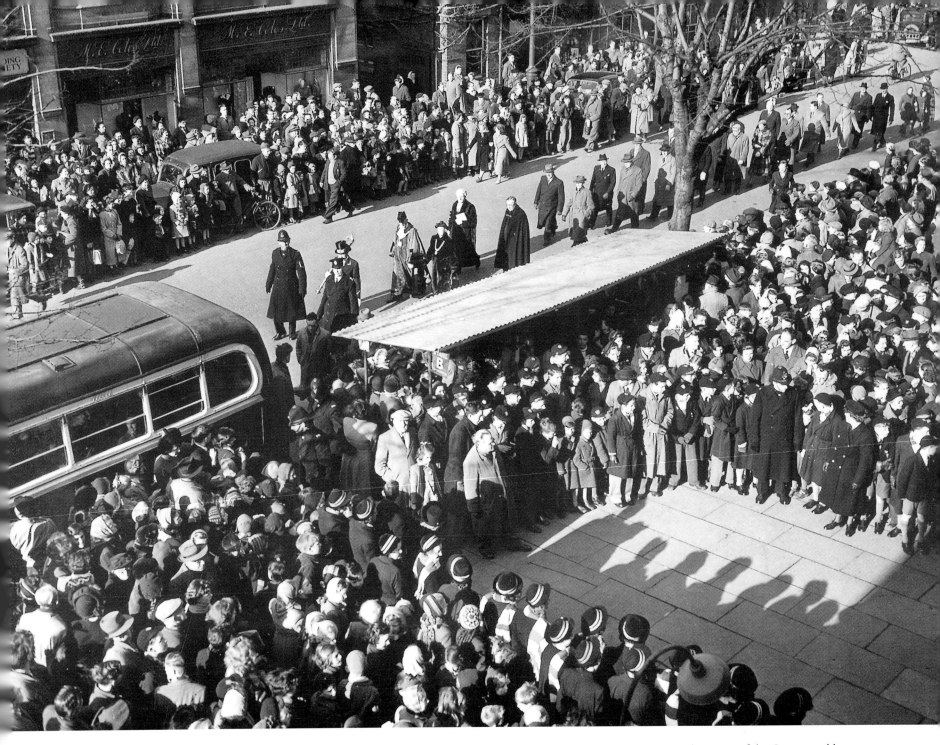

Huge crowds thronged the street outside Kettering Library at noon on Saturday, 9 February 1952 to hear the Proclamation of the Queen read by the Mayor, Ald. Charles Goode (see next page). Surrounded by members of the town council, he gave the address from the library steps, his voice carried by loudspeakers to the hundreds who had gathered in Sheep Street half an hour earlier, stopping the traffic. Hundreds more had followed the Mayoral procession from the council offices. Afterwards the crowd sang "God Save The Queen" to a musical recording. Princess Elizabeth ascended the throne following the death of her father, King George VI, but was not crowned until the following year. Kettering's Proclamation ceremony was held a day later than most other towns in the area so that workers and schoolchildren could attend. (*Judy Eden*)

Alderman Goode (1892-1973)

Alderman Charles Edward Goode, seen here reading the Proclamation of the Queen in 1952, was the "grand old man" of Kettering Council. Known as "Ted" to friends, he served on the council from 1937 until his death on 3 July 1973 (even attending the finance committee meeting the night before). He was Mayor in 1951/52, deputy the following year and again in 1957. He was made Freeman of the Borough in 1970 – only the third person to be so honoured. Born in Market Harborough but brought up in Kettering, he served for four years on the Western Front with the Northants Regiment during World War I. By trade a printer, he was governor of Kettering Grammar School, Kettering High School and the Technical College, a former chairman of Kettering Operatic Society, and chaired the Kettering TB Care Committee for 18 years. He was also a member of the Nene River Board, Mid-Northants Water Board, Great Ouse Water Board and the British Waterworks Association. His prime concern was to see that the county had an adequate water supply. (*Judy Eden*)

Jim Dale

Do you recognise this fresh-faced young man wowing the women at Coles footwear factory in Burton Latimer in May 1958? Yes, it's none other than Jim Dale, the former Kettering Grammar School pupil who later became star of the stage and screen, best known for his appearances in the classic Carry On films. Known as plain Jim Smith in his native Rothwell, Jim was "discovered" in a talent show at Kettering's former Savoy Theatre and made his TV debut alongside the legendary Max Miller. When this picture was taken with shoe worker Shirley Knibbs (the firm was designing a shoe bearing his name), he was a Fifties singing star and heart-throb host of the hit TV pop show *Six-Five Special*. Jim had wanted to go on the stage since his mum entered him in dance classes (my aunt was one of his dance partners). As a singer he enjoyed a few chart hits and wrote the song *Georgy Girl* for the Seekers, but he made his name as the star of ten *Carry On* films in the 1960s. Now living in New York, he won a Tony Award for his title role in the hit Broadway musicasl Barnum and more recently he played Fagin in *Oliver!* at the London Palladium. When I met him in 1992 at the Leicester Square premiere of *Carry On Columbus* (the first *Carry On* film for 24 years), Jim was delighted to chat to another Grammar School "old boy" and kept other journalists waiting as he quizzed me about the latest progress in the building of the A1-M1 link road (now the A14)! (*Kettering Leader and Guardian*)

Richard Coles

When Kettering keyboard wizard Richard Coles (with the glasses) teamed up with singer Jimmy Somerville to form the pop band The Communards, the duo became one of the musical success stories of the 1980s. Richard is the son of Nigel Coles, former boss of Coles Boot Company (see previous page) and past president of Kettering Chamber of Trade. A classically trained pianist, he was brought up in Ridgeway Road, Barton Seagrave, went to St Peter's School, Kettering, then became a day boarder at Wellingborough School until he was 16. The Communards had a string of hit singles, including *You Are My World*, *Never Can Say Goodbye* and the chart-topping *Don't Leave Me This Way*. Richard later launched a new career, winning Best New Broadcaster of the Year at the 1992 Sony Music Awards for his own late-night show The Mix on Radio 5. Two bass guitarists with Kettering connections have also been chart-toppers. Horace Panter (whom I knew from Kettering Grammar School in the late 1960s) played with The Specials on their two No.1 hits, *Too Much Too Young* and *Ghost Town*. The other is former Kettering Technical College student John Illsley, who co-founded Dire Straits with Mark Knopfler and is a multi-millionaire! (*London Records*)

Keystone Boys Club

The Keystone Skiffle Group pictured in the gardens of Wicksteed Park during the late 1950s. Its six members belonged to Keystone Boys' Club and found nationwide fame by appearing on the cult TV pop show *Six-Five Special*. The club was formed in 1956 after a meeting of local businessmen at the Central Hall. In its heyday in the 1960s Keystone was open five nights a week, offering a wide range of sporting facilities to its 200 members aged 13 to 21. After spells at the Hare and Hounds pub and Seneschal House in Wadcroft, the club found a permanent home at Grosvenor House in Rockingham Road. Now renamed Keystone Youth Centre, it is open to both boys and girls from the age of nine upwards. (*John Barton*)

Members of Keystone Boys' Club aboard their float at Kettering Carnival during the 1960s. The carnival replaced the annual Hospital Parade and celebrated its 50th anniversary in 1998. It is organised by members of the Kettering and District Amalgamated Clubs' Committee for the Blind and its first parade, which left Headlands and ended at the Poppies football ground, raised £1,000. Various venues have been used over the years, from the old agricultural show ground off Patrick Road to Avondale School playing fields and Northampton Road recreation ground. In recent times the carnival has departed from the Grange Estate and ended at Rockingham Road Pleasure Park. The first carnival queen, elected in 1955, was Brenda Bennett and since 1973 the carnival queen from Kettering's German twin-town of Lahnstein has taken part. (*Chronicle and Echo*)

Frankie Vaughan

Pop singer Frankie Vaughan chats to members of Keystone Boys' Club and their friends in the balcony of the Central Hall during a dance in aid of the club on Friday, 26 October 1962. Much to the delight of his fans, he performed two songs, including one of his early hits, *Green Door*, before receiving a £500 cheque from the club's Supporters Association and passsing it on to club chairman Mr J. Mackay. The Kettering visit was part of a lightning tour of the area that day. His first stop was Corby where he opened the new Woodnewton Boys' Club, signed autographs, and had a cup of tea at the Spread Eagle Hotel with officials from the Northamptonshire Association of Boys' Clubs. He later dined at Kettering's George Hotel and after the dance he left for Northampton to attend a function arranged by the town's Kings Heath Adventure Club. I must confess here that the first single I ever bought as a young boy of seven was Frankie's 1961 hit *Tower of Strength*. From his TV appearances I always imagined him to be a big macho guy, at least 6ft tall, but when I interviewed him at another boys' club event at Wicksteed Park in 1972, he was disappointingly several inches shorter. (*John Barton*)

Actor Wilfred Brambell, best known as TV rag-and-bone man Albert Steptoe, stops to chat at the Palmer's Music Stores stand during a visit to the Kettering Chamber of Trade Exhibition at Wicksteed Park on 1 October 1963. Mr Brambell officially opened the event before an enthusiastic and largely young audience which packed the park's cinema. This dapper man in a smart grey suit admitted he had passed through Kettering a number of times, but this was the first time he had stopped off in the town. After presenting the cup for the best trade display to grocers T. A. Cobley and Son, he was himself presented with a shoe box containing a pair of old boots for which even Harold Steptoe would not give threepence. Everybody roared at the joke, but before the laughter had died down, a genuine pair of Kettering-made shoes were produced, which Wilfred immediately tried on. A second surprise presentation was of a carved wooden fruit bowl Mr Brambell had admired on the stand of furnishers F. A. Watts. Being a starstruck young lad, I joined hundreds of children who queued up for the star's autograph (see inset), not because of *Steptoe and Son* but because he had just played Paul McCartney's grandfather in the Beatles' first film, *A Hard Day's Night!* (*Kettering Leader*)

Friday, 9 July 1965 was a memorable day for Kettering when the Queen and Duke of Edinburgh visited the town as part of a seven-hour tour of the county. I remember being one of thousands of schoolchildren who lined the Royal route waving their Union Jacks as the couple drove past en route to Satra House in Rockingham Road (well, we were excused classes that morning). The Queen and Duke were greeted by Kettering Mayor, Ald. Ernest Crayford and his wife Vera, pictured here escorting their guests to the Art Gallery to meet council members and see the model of Kettering's proposed new town centre. Then it was on to Satra House for a guided tour of the footwear research centre. The Queen, looking resplendent in her yellow outfit, then departed with her husband for further visits to Higham Ferrers, Wellingborough and Northampton. The *Northamptonshire Advertiser* series, which included the weekly papers, the *Kettering Leader* and *Wellingborough News*, published a special 16-page colour supplement as a souvenir of the day. Alderman Crayford, who retired in 1977 after 19 years' service on Kettering Council, moved to Brighton with his wife in 1983 to be nearer their daughter. He died in a nursing home at Worthing in August 1998, aged 92.
(*Northamptonshire Advertiser*)

Kettering Grammar School

When the former Kettering Grammar School closed in 1994 because of falling rolls, it was the end of more than 400 years of history. Indeed many traditionalists among its "old boys" and teachers felt the writing was on the wall the moment the school, founded in 1577, merged with Stamford Road Secondary School to become Kettering Boys' School in 1976. Its impressive alumni ranged from the town's famous missionary and slavery abolitionist William Knibb (1803-1849) to home-grown artists Sir Alfred East (1849-1913) and Thomas Cooper Gotch (1855-1931). The late Rushden author H. E. Bates, whose books inspired the hit TV series *The Darling Buds of May*, was a pupil during World War I. A less illustrious writer – yours truly – was a third-former when this official school photograph was taken in April 1968 and may be spotted on the left of the back row (circled) with regulation "pudding basin" haircut (minus the specs and beard, of course).

My apologies to those lads on the far left and right of this scrolled picture, inevitable victims of the picture cropping process, but for the record, here are the names of the school's 40 teachers (complete with their class nicknames to help jog memories): Seated from left to right are: John ("Joe") Beales, Tom Welch, Les Berridge, Frank ("Tufty") Thompson, Geoff ("Gus") Phillips, Idwall ("Nailer") Jones, Newton ("Nerve") Jones, Geoff ("Bumble") Perry, Paul Sharpling, Cliff Brown, Maurice Till, Ray Perryman, Brian ("Bill") Perrett, Bob Jones, Derek ("Slasher") Slater, Evan ("Ted") Roberts, John ("Tarzan") Cowell, David Fox, Tony Simmons, Dick Rattley, Paul ("Prim") Morris, John Steane (headmaster), Russell ("Reggie") Gladden, Jack ("Joey") Young, Brian Barker, Ivor Welch, Noel ("Bertie") Holland, David ("Cat") Stephens, Ieuan ("Taffy") Layton-Matthews, Derek Wade, John ("Stick") Marshall, Barry Wright, Stephen ("Jet") Harris, Ken ("Chip") Mandale, Gordon ("Jock") Brown, John Gibson, David Bone, Richard Lambert, John Larcombe, John Jackson. The two secretaries also pictured are Mrs Doreen Stebbings and Mrs Connie Phillips. I am advised not to publish the nickname of the headmaster to avoid possible legal action! (*Tony Smith*)

The former KGS building in Windmill Avenue is now the Tresham Sixth Form Centre.
(*Tony Smith*)

Joe Starmer (1890-1961)

Boxing legend Joe Starmer (far left) carried the name of Kettering to all corners of the globe. Heavyweight Jack Johnson once called him "The greatest little fighting machine I have ever seen."

In the early part of the century Joe mixed it with men like Ted "Kid" Lewis, Jimmy Wilde, Jim Driscoll and Bombardier Billy Wells – all household names. But he never quite made the top – he was Midlands Featherweight Champion and fought for the Great Britain and European titles, but they eluded him.

Born Ernest Samuel Starmer at Kettering in 1890, he was admired as a "gentleman" of the ring, and in 1910 began his systematic demolition of opponents, despite being 5ft 3in in his stockinged feet and 5lb under 10 stone in fighting trim. He disposed of eight fighters that year, including points victories over "Boyo" Driscoll and French champion Eugene Trickri. At the height of his fame he lost to "Kid" Lewis in an eliminator for the GB Championship and Lonsdale Belt and in 1914 was beaten by Louis de Pontieu for the European title in Paris.

Renowned for his "tearaway" style, Joe once thrashed Tommy Mitchell in two minutes to win the Midlands title.

War interrupted his career but he made a brief comeback in 1927 before going into the haulage business. He started one of Kettering's earliest garages in Windmill Avenue and ended his working days as a bus driver with United Counties. The man on the right of the picture is Vaudeville boxer Joey Smith. (*Tony Smith*)

David Steele

County cricket hero David Steele was one of the best loved sporting heroes adopted by the people of Kettering. Born in Stoke-on-Trent, "Steeley" came from a cricketing family, his uncle being the Lancs and Staffs all-rounder Stanley Crump, who played the game until he was 60. He moved to Northants in 1963, making the first of 30 centuries against Essex. But his expected England call did not come until 1975 – at the age of 34. Then living in Kettering, this bespectacled, silver-haired veteran became a national hero overnight after hitting 50 against the Aussies at Lords. He capped a remarkable season by winning the coveted BBC Sports Personality of the Year trophy (pictured). David played in eight tests for England, scoring 673 runs in 16 innings, his best being 106 against the West Indies at Trent Bridge. When he hung up his pads in 1983, aged 43, he had played in 500 first class matches, scoring a total of 22,346 runs and 30 centuries. For Northants he scored 18,231 runs in 416 matches, taking 462 wickets and 469 catches. David, who used to work for Staples Printers in Kettering, later moved to Geddington and even today he is sometimes stopped in the street by fans who still remember the days when he was Kettering's "*Boys' Own*" Hero". (*Evening Telegraph*)

Amy Johnson Conquers Kettering.

Charmingly Told Story of Epic Flight to Australia in "Jason."

ADVENTURES THRILLING & HUMOROUS.

ALL SMILES.—An interesting picture of Amy standing beside "Jason III" just before leaving Glendon on Saturday. Mr. A. Joyce (general manager of the Kettering Co-operative Society) conveyed to Amy the warmest wishes of the company gathered at the "take-off" for a pleasant "hop" to Sywell.

Kettering crowds brought traffic to a standstill when pioneering aviator Amy Johnson visited the town on Friday, 9 October 1931. The intrepid Miss Johnson, who had recently completed a record solo flight to Australia, was invited by Kettering Industrial Co-operative Society to give an illustrated talk about her latest adventure. When she arrived at the Central Hall, the Queen of the Air was mobbed by cheering fans who blocked Montagu Street, and was welcomed inside by a band playing the jazz song Amy, written in her honour. After a reception by local VIPS, she enthralled her audience with details of her flight to the "Land of the Golden Fleece" before staying the night at the Kettering home of Alderman Mrs Frances Clarke. Miss Johnson had arrived late for her lecture after fog prevented her landing her Tiger Moth at Sywell aerodrome, the plane later touching down in a field near Rushton. While waiting for a car from Kettering to pick her up, she had a cup of tea with two startled railway workers at a nearby signal box! The next day the legendary flyer visited the new KICS Central Stores and offices in King Street, where she received gifts from her many admirers on the staff. After lunch at Sywell, waving crowds watched her take off for London and her next engagement. Miss Johnson, who also made record solo flights to America, Japan and the Cape (twice), died ten years later, presumed drowned after her plane crashed into the Thames Estuary.
(*Kettering Leader and Guardian*)

Kettering Town Football Club

In 1997 Kettering Town Football Club celebrated its 125th anniversary and the centenary of playing at its Rockingham Road ground. The club was formed in 1872, turned professional in 1891, and played in a dozen different leagues before becoming founder members of the Football Alliance in 1979 (later the GM Vauxhall Conference). Its first home was Eldred's Field, south of Green Lane (now the York Road and Tennyson Road area), before moving to North Park for a short spell. In the early days the team competed against the likes of Tottenham Hotspur, West Ham, Aston Villa, Southampton and QPR. When Spurs won the FA Cup after a replay in 1901, they completed their league programme by drawing 1-1 at Rockingham Road! Pictured here is the Poppies team which played in the Central Alliance in 1920/21. New signings included the popular ex-Crystal Palace captain Harry Hanger and Swansea outside right Fred Harris (that season the grandstand was altered to seven tiers instead of five, costing almost £100). Standing from left to right are F. Dexter (trainer), F. W. Smith, Percy Hanger, Summerley, Walker, Bellamy, Loasby, Harry Hanger (captain) and Arthur Hanger (secretary). Seated are F. Burditt (chairman), F. M. Harris, Basson, Heeley, Roberts, Upton, Austin and Charles Farron (committee member). Forward F. W. Smith, for some reason, was known as "Danky". (*Tony Smith*)

Tommy Lawton (1919-1996)

Helga Tye's "exclusive" picture of Arsenal and England legend Tommy Lawton signing for the Poppies "live" on the BBC's *Sportsview* programme on Wednesday, 1 February 1956. Kettering paid £1,000 for the bustling centre-forward, who had scored more than 250 goals in senior football and 22 goals in 23 appearances for his country. As player-manager, he steered the Poppies to the Southern League championship (watched by an average home crowd of 4,000!) before returning to the Football League as manager of Notts County. When I interviewed Tommy on his 69th birthday, he told me that leaving Kettering, where he became a folk hero, was his biggest regret. Sadly he had fallen on hard times (in retirement he had to sell his medals and England caps to make ends meet). Tommy was the Alan Shearer of his day but without his million pound wages (he earned £17 a week in the First Division). Pictured with him here are Poppies secretary Frank Summerley, chairman Reg Tailby and a young David Coleman.

Another England all-time great who once wore a Poppies shirt was full-back Eddie Hapgood, whom Kettering sold to Arsenal for £1,000 in 1927. Hapgood (inset) was in the great Gunners side of the 1930s, winning the First Division five times and the FA Cup twice.
(Kettering Leader and Guardian)

WILLS'S CIGARETTES

THIS SURFACE IS ADHESIVE. ASK YOUR TOBACCONIST FOR THE ATTRACTIVE ALBUM (PRICE ONE PENNY) SPECIALLY PREPARED TO HOLD THE COMPLETE SERIES

ASSOCIATION FOOTBALLERS
A SERIES OF 50
19
E. HAPGOOD
(Arsenal)

England's captain and the Arsenal's left back, Hapgood has won every honour the game offers —four League championship medals, a Cup-winner's medal and six consecutive international caps at home since 1934. He has also appeared against six foreign countries as well as against Scotland in the Jubilee match in Aug. 1935. Trained in junior football in Bristol, he was discovered by the Arsenal at Kettering, and he was obtained in October 1927 for a small fee; he quickly developed into one of the best backs in the game. Slightly built, he succeeds by his quick anticipation and all round cleverness rather than by any display of force, and he is an excellent kick.

W.D. & H.O. WILLS
ISSUED BY THE IMPERIAL TOBACCO CO. (OF GREAT BRITAIN & IRELAND), LTD.

E. HAPGOOD (ARSENAL)

CHAMPIONS !

The Poppies team which won the Southern League Premier Division title in 1973, under Ron Atkinson (later to become a successful manager at Manchester United, Barcelona and Aston Villa, to name just a few of his clubs). The players standing are Dick Dighton, Vincent O'Kane, Brian Myton, Ray Webster, Roger Ashby, Joe Kiernan and Trevor Peck. Crouching at the front are George Cleary, Roy Clayton, Mick Goodall and Colin Harrington. Other squad members that season included Colin Mackleworth, John Pawley, Mick Reed and Big Ron himself. I have been an ardent but long-suffering Poppies fan since the age of seven, when my late father took me to see their first floodlit match at Rockingham Road on Monday, 9 October 1961. Before the inaugural game there was a short concert by the Munn and Felton Band (see page 143) and the new lights were then officially switched on by Sir Stanley Rous, secretary of the Football Association. We drew 2-2 with an Ipswich Town side (then managed by a certain Alf Ramsey) which went on to win the First Division championship that season. The Ipswich centre-forward that night was Ray Crawford who, before that decade was over, signed for Kettering. Ray notched up 23 goals in 37 appearances for the Poppies before returning to the Football League and going on to score two vital goals in Colchester United's famous FA Cup victory over First Division Leeds United in 1971. Kettering's own giant-killing exploits in the FA Cup have included wins over Oxford United, Millwall, Swindon and Bristol Rovers, the latter game featured on BBC's *Match of the Day* in 1988. The Poppies' FA Cup home defeat against Plymouth Argyle in 1994 was broadcast "live" on Sky TV. (*Evening Telegraph*)

Return from Wembley, 1979

There were amazing scenes in Kettering on Monday, 22 May 1979 when thousands of fans turned out to greet the Poppies' return from Wembley. Two days earlier Kettering became a ghost town as Mick Jones' team lost 2-0 to Stafford Rangers in the FA Trophy final before a then-record non-league crowd of 32,000. That Saturday, 42 coaches, two special trains and hundreds of cars made their way to the famous twin towers. Although the team didn't return with the cup, they were given a hero's welcome as they did a lap of honour around the town aboard an open-top bus. All along the mile-and-a-half route from the old cattle market to the Rockingham Road ground, there was a sea of red and white, with people hanging out of windows, standing on top of phone boxes and dancing in the street. A deafening roar greeted the players as the bus turned into the crowded club car park and police struggled to keep the huge crowd at bay. The players, who were given a civic reception, received rapturous applause as they leaned out of the upstairs window at the Bowling Green, and supporters, many of them weeping with emotion, stayed on after dark to get autographs from their heroes. The most memorable match in recent times was in 1989 when the Poppies came so close to reaching the Fifth Round of the FA Cup. More than 8,000 fans travelled to Selhurst Park to witness the 2-1 defeat by First Division Charlton Athletic, with only the width of a post denying veteran striker Ernie Moss a deserved equaliser in the last minute. The record gate at Rockingham Road was the 11,526 squeezed in for an FA Cup tie against long-time rivals Peterborough in 1947. They witnessed a thrilling game, which the Poppies lost 4-3 after missing a last-minute penalty. That day's attendance will never be beaten as the ground's capacity has been reduced to just over 6,000 for safety reasons.

(*Evening Telegraph*)

Tony Ireson

My good friend and mentor Tony Ireson pictured outside Beech Cottage in March 1972, when his historic home in Tanners Lane was threatened by the Gold Street redevelopment plans. The veteran writer and historian won a personal battle with Kettering Council, who wanted to demolish the eighteenth-century building (where he has lived since 1947) to create a service road to the new multi-storey car park. Like myself, Tony is Kettering born and bred, joining the *Evening Telegraph* from Kettering Grammar School. During his 30 years on the paper, he became the authoritative voice on his native county, writing a best-selling book on Northamptonshire in 1954 (the year I was born!). Tony is a founder member of Kettering Civic Society and in retirement wrote the compelling book *Old Kettering and its Defenders*, a detailed and definitive account of the bitter battle over the town centre redevelopment in the 1970s. Now in his mid-80s, he remains tireless in his quest to publish as much about Kettering's history as mortality will allow, with six volumes of townspeople's memories already under his belt (despite arthritis and limited mobility). I highly recommend to those who have enjoyed reading this book Tony's excellent series on Kettering in the 1930s. (*Evening Telegraph*)

Frank Bellamy (1917-1976)

Kit Mallin's photograph of the brilliant comic book illustrator Frank Bellamy in his studio at home shortly before his death from a heart attack at the age of 59. Kettering-born Frank was a master craftsman and an artist in the truest sense of the word. His career began drawing film posters for Kettering cinemas and weekly cartoons for the *Pink 'Un*, the *Evening Telegraph*'s Saturday sports paper, in the 1940s. But he made his name during the 1950s and early 1960s working for the legendary *Eagle* comic, producing the serialised life stories of Winston Churchill and Montgomery of Alamein in comic strip form. Both masterpieces were painstakingly researched, the first approved by Churchill himself before going into print. Frank drew the award-winning action adventure *Heros the Spartan*, took over and revamped *Dan Dare* when his creator Frank Hampson took a year's sabbatical, and pioneered the use of limited colour with his *Frazer of Africa* strip. Bellamy went on to draw the cult *Thunderbirds* strip for TV 21, the daily *Garth* fantasy strip for the *Daily Mirror*, and was the first graphic artist to illustrate the *Sunday Times* colour supplement. I became friendly with Frank just months before he died and was the last journalist to interview him. He was extraordinarily modest about his own genius and almost childlike in his enthusiasm for his craft. We first met when I interviewed him for an *ET* feature, expecting it would take half an hour. I was so engrossed I was there for SIX HOURS! (*Evening Telegraph*)

Arthur Heath

The name of Arthur Heath (left) has probably appeared in the columns of the *Evening Telegraph* more times than my own in recent history! Arthur was a founder member of Kettering Civic Society, formed at the Manor House on 9 June 1969, and this year marked his 30th as chairman. His hard work and dedication to improving the town and protecting its heritage earned him an MBE in the 1995 New Year's honours list, presented by John Lowther, the county's Lord Lieutenant, at an official ceremony at the George Hotel. With Arthur at the helm, the society has published several booklets and postcards on Kettering's history and has campaigned constantly to preserve its buildings of character. Its biggest and most bitter battle was over Gold Street redevelopment in the 1970s, which led to a controversial public inquiry and failure to save Beech House and the Post Office block from the bulldozers. Since then the Civic Society has presented an annual award for the most deserving environmental project in the town. Arthur, who lives in Roundhill Road with his charming wife Evelyn, is also acknowledged as a world expert on electric kettles (!) and for many years has served as secretary of Kettering Book Society, originally formed in 1808 to preserve and promote literature. And no, he wasn't a founder member!

Simon Thornton (1935-1997)

I was very saddened when Kettering business and community stalwart Simon Thornton (right) died so suddenly. I had known him for over 25 years and, being a motoring enthusiast, he helped identify old vehicles featured in my last book. Since 1960 he had run the family jewellers shop founded by his grandfather Arthur (Kettering's second mayor) and continued by his own father Pat, who died in 1978. Simon became president of Kettering Rotary Club in 1980, 14 years after his father, and was a member of the Royal British Legion, the district car club and scouting movement. He was also an active member of the Chamber of Trade and Kettering Town Centre Partnership. Professionally, he was chairman of the National Association of Valuers, a senior warden of the Worshipful Company of Clockmakers and founder chairman of the National Association of Goldsmiths. Hundreds of mourners packed Kettering Parish Church for his funeral in 1997 and the main address was given by former *ET* editor Ron Hunt. A memorial plaque was unveiled at Kettering Conservative Club in 1998.

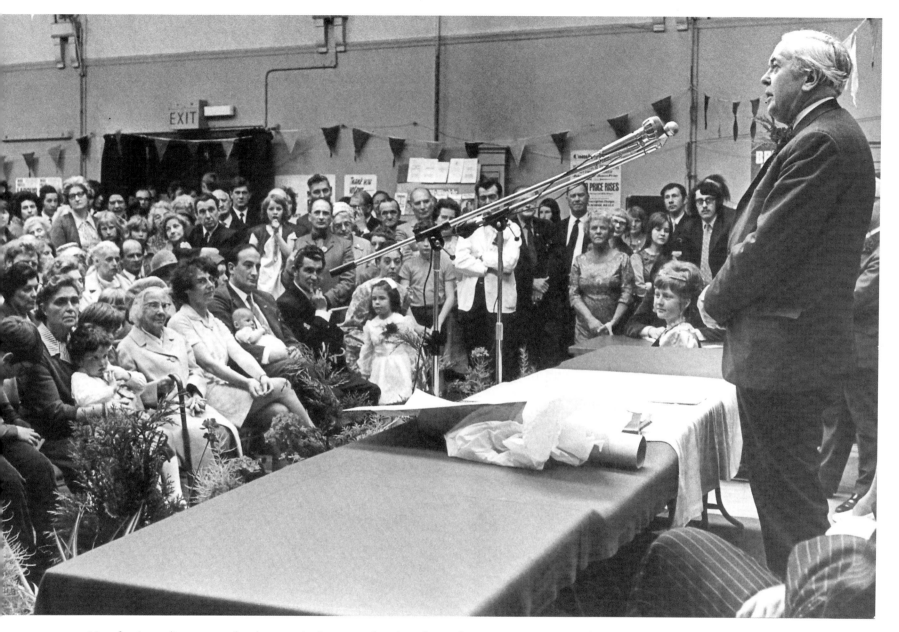

Very few journalists can say they have received a personal apology from a former Prime Minister. When Harold Wilson paid a flying visit to open Kettering Labour Party's summer fair on Saturday, 19 June 1972, he accidentally trod on my foot moving through the crowd at the Corn Market Hall! Mr Wilson, then Opposition leader, made a 30-minute stop en route from Derby to Wellingborough to slam the record of the Conservative government, which celebrated the end of its second year in office that weekend. On his first visit to the town, he was given a civic welcome outside the hall by the Mayor and Mayoress, Alderman and Mrs David Thompson, and greeted inside by Kettering MP Sir Geoffrey de Freitas. After being introduced to local supporters by Kettering Labour Party chairman Ray Cross, Mr Wilson was presented with an illuminated copy of the town's coat of arms and charter. The former premier was also given an illustrated map of his home county of Yorkshire by Kettering artist and author J. L. Carr (see next page) and received a bouquet from four-year-old Dawn Gosland, daughter of town councillor Kenneth Gosland. Eagle-eyed readers may spot a rather long-haired junior reporter standing to Harold's right. (*Kettering Leader*)

J. L. Carr (1912-1994)

Kettering headmaster turned top novelist James Lloyd Carr died at his Mill Dale Road home in February 1994, aged 81. Known in print as J. L. Carr, but to friends as Jim, he had several of his works adapted for television and two novels shortlisted for the Booker Prize. Yorkshire-born Mr Carr came to Kettering after the war, taught briefly at Kettering Grammar School and became head teacher at Highfield Primary School. In retirement he took up writing and was a regular essayist and critic for *The Guardian* and *The Spectator*. *A Day in Summer*, his first novel in 1963, was filmed for Yorkshire TV and *A Month in the Country*, shortlisted for the Booker Prize, became a Channel 4 film. Also shortlisted was *The Battle For Pollocks Crossing*, while *How Steeple Sinderby Wanderers Won The FA Cup* was staged at the Mermaid Theatre in London. Mr Carr, who set up his own publishing company, printing 230 books, was a talented stone-carver and his figures of the Virgin and Child can be found in Kettering Parish Church. He was also an accomplished artist and enjoyed several one-man exhibitions of his work.
(*Evening Telegraph*)

Fred Moore (1915–1999)

No book on the history of Kettering would be complete without paying tribute to the undisputed expert on the town, Fred Moore, who sadly died in June 1999 at the age of 83. Dear old Fred had an encyclopaedic knowledge of Kettering, having amassed in his lifetime an astonishing collection of photographs and local memorabilia. He is probably best remembered for his popular "magic lantern" shows of old Kettering, using a modified 1905 lantern (pictured right) to project glass slides originally owned by local photographer Warren East. Born in Duke Street, Fred's working life began as a 14-year-old latherboy at Flude's barbers in Princes Street, but Kettering people will know him as a second-hand book dealer and record dealer for more than four decades. Under the name F. A. Moore, his first shop opened in Market Street in 1948, moving to Montagu Street in 1962, his wife Gladys helping out on Saturdays (their marriage lasted 60 years). When I was a young boy brought up in Elizabeth Road, Fred – who lived on the corner of Judith Road – cut a familar figure riding to and from his shop by bike, even coming home for lunch. Sadly poor health forced Fred to give up the shop and his slide shows, which gave so much pleasure to Kettering people and raised more than £1,000 for charity. The bookshop continues to trade, now run by Mrs Brenda Wise. (*Evening Telegraph*)

John Nash (1927-1990)

Local tycoon John Nash, millionaire chairman of the Poppies for 21 years, was the man with the Midas touch. The business and political career of this former Kettering Grammar School pupil made him as well known as his long association with Kettering Town Football Club. He followed in his father's footsteps by becoming a chartered accountant and in the mid-1960s set up his own hugely successful accountancy business in Station Road. When J. F. Nash Securities went public in 1972, it was valued at £2 million and controlled the finances of 100 companies and subsidiaries. One of his greatest achievements was rescuing the ailing Reliant Motors group. His burning ambition was to take Kettering Town into the Football League, bringing such big name player-managers as Ron Atkinson and Derek Dougan to the club, but resigned after one too many near-misses under the old election system. John stood as Tory candidate for Kettering in the 1955 General Election but lost, declaring he had no money and would give up politics, but he continued to play an active role with Kettering Council and the County Council, which made him an Alderman in 1970. (*Evening Telegraph*)

THE
REG. CIVIL
SCHOOL OF DANCING
LIBERAL CLUB
Dalkeith Place, Kettering
Also at :—
THE PUBLIC HALL, CORBY

BALLROOM DANCING. Latest Dances, Variations and Style, as danced in the Leading London Dance Halls.
OPERATIC DANCING taught by the methods required by the Operatic Association of Great Britain.
TAP DANCING. All Styles, Step, Buck, Schottische, etc.

National, Ballet, Character, Musical Comedy, Limbering and Acrobatic.

Special Dances arranged to suit Pupils' requirements

Delicate children receive special attention

PRIVATE LESSONS BY APPOINTMENT

'Phone **2402**

Reg Civil (1913-1978)

Kettering's tap-dancing comedian Reg Civil trod the boards of Britain's old variety theatres during the 1940s and 1950s after running a successful dance school, which began in Gordon Street in 1936 and continued in the ballroom on the top floor of the Liberal Club. Reg, once dubbed Kettering's Fred Astaire, was raised in Russell Street by his grandmother after his parents, tragically, both died of tuberculosis following World War I (when his father was gassed in the trenches). An entertainer of the old school, Reg was a leading light with Kettering Operatic and Kettering and District Theatrical Society before teaming up professionally with Bill Green as the crazy Lynton Boys, an eccentric dance and tumbling act. During World War II he served as a physical training instructor with the RAF and married Sybil (Tyrrell) in 1940. The Lynton Boys once performed on the same bill as their heroes, The Crazy Gang, and Reg did a summer season at Colwyn Bay with Max Bygraves. He also teamed up with Arthur Remington and Cyril Fairey to become The Three Toppers and finally formed a double act with local singer Johnny Williams called Civil and Connell. In his long career Reg also played alongside Sam Costa, Charlie Chester, Ray Ellington and Petula Clark but his dancing days were curtailed after Boxing Day 1960, when both his legs were badly broken in a car crash. One of his pupils during his dance school days was Rothwell's Jim Dale (see page 146), who admitted using steps taught by Reg when playing Fagin in the musical *Oliver!* at the London Palladium a few years ago. Poppies fans also knew Reg as the Tannoy announcer at Rockingham Road and he also worked as an MC for Keystone Boys' Club at local boxing matches and toastmaster at dinners and dances. These last two roles are continued by his showbiz son Bobby, an Equity member who has enjoyed walk-on parts in such TV series as *Emmerdale*, *Casualty*, *The Bill* and *House of Elliot*. Reg's daughter Nathia is married to Kettering financier and former Poppies director Terry Gray. (*Nathia Gray*)

Bob and Eileen Denney (1914-1998)

Alderman Bob and Eileen Denney, pictured here as Mayor and Mayoress of Kettering in 1968. were influential figures in both the town's development and in the community. Bob, director of Thursfields chemists, was elected to Kettering Council in 1961 and awarded the MBE in 1992 for his public service. He is a former secretary of Kettering Chamber of Trade, chairman of Age Concern and the business group Probus, and president of Kettering Men's and Women's Own. Ironically, when Mayor, Kettering Civic Society was formed on his proposal, but both came into conflict when Bob later chaired the planning committee during the Gold Street redevelopment controversy (even opposing his wife over the fate of Beech House and Beech Cottage). Eileen was councillor for Kingsley Ward for 21 years, chaired the amenities and recreation committee and oversaw the development of the new swimming pool in London Road. She was president of Kettering Liberal Association, chairman of Kettering Townswomen's Guild and the local branch of Cancer Relief, losing her second battle with the disease in January 1998, a year before she and Bob were due to celebrate their diamond wedding.
(*Kettering Leader*)

8. Later Years

The snow-covered playground of the old Parish Church School in Horsemarket pictured during the big freeze of 1963, when thermometers at Kettering dropped to an all-time low. After almost a month of wintry weather, there was a furious blizzard on Saturday, 19 January and within just a few hours minor roads were blocked, bus services halted and main roads reduced to single lane by huge drifts. That morning there were 12 degrees of frost, but by Tuesday, 22 January this had risen to 26 and then 32 on the Wednesday, when this picture was taken. Hundreds of schoolchildren enjoyed a bonus holiday and local coal merchants and shops selling paraffin were kept busy! The Poppies, then managed by Wally Akers, had been without a match for four weeks. Arguments have since raged over which winter was worst – 1916, 1945 or 1963. What is certain is that when this picture was taken it was the coldest day since records began. The freeze continued throughout February that year, causing heating problems for schools, factories, shops and greenhouse owners. It was not until 6 March that locals enjoyed the first frost-free night since 22 December the previous year. (*Kettering Leader*)

This was the chaotic scene in Bowling Green Road during one of Kettering's worst ever traffic jams on Sunday, 17 May 1964. Believe it or not, this queue of vehicles tailed right back down London Road from Wicksteed Park, which was forced to close its gates for 20 minutes for the first time in its history. Record crowds also flocked there the following day – the Whitsun Bank Holiday – as the sun blazed down. Saturday saw a taste of what was to come when ice cream sales were the best of the season, though Sunday's sales topped them. Sunday's traffic build-up began in the morning and by 1.30pm the main car park was a third full. By 4pm there was just the odd space left and 15 minutes later the "car parks full" notice went up until stewards had guided one stream of traffic out. Just over 5,600 cars were in the park during the day, some even on the cycle track and the pony field! Buses travelling on routes past the park to and from Rushden and Burton Latimer or Kettering town centre were delayed for up to half an hour. During the morning of Bank Holiday Monday, more than 1,500 people came into Kettering off trains from Leicester en route to "Wickies" and many hundreds more packed the station to catch special trains to Hunstanton. But, unlike some seaside resorts, there were no brawls between teenage hooligans at Wicksteed Park (marauding youths left a trail of havoc at Margate and Brighton that same weekend). The most popular attraction in the hot weather was the famous "water chute", with a steady queue of day trippers trying to cool down, and at one point the queue for the miniature railway was as long as the station. (*Kettering Leader*)

Kettering Furnaces

All steamed up for action is one of the three-foot gauge trains that used to carry ore to and from Kettering Furnaces. For the best part of 80 years the furnaces lit up the night sky alongside the railway off Rockingham Road and at the height of production employed some 600 men (see page 43). Pictured here in its final days is fleet veteran No. 2 Engine, made by Black, Hawthorn and Company in 1879. Kettering Iron and Coal Company once owned a dozen 0-4-0 and 0-6-0 locomotives to ferry the ironstone from local pits, plus one double-ended engine with two upright boilers. (*Tony Smith*)

Kettering Furnaces closed in 1959, and when they were demolished in 1963 the Kettering Iron and Coal Company presented this narrow gauge Manning Wardle locomotive (No. 8 Engine) to the town council. The engine, built in 1906, is pictured here being gently rolled from a transporter on to a special strip of track outside the Manor House on 26 August 1963. Original plans for it to be protected under cover were abandoned because of lack of funds and it became so dilapidated that in 1973 Kettering Council loaned it to the Welland Valley Vintage Traction Club on a care and maintenance basis and, I'm told, it hopes to have it up and running early in the new millennium. Local train buffs should visit the excellent little museum at Irchester Country Park run by the Irchester Narrow Gauge Railway Trust. Since 1988 dedicated enthusiasts have restored several old locomotives used in county quarries to pristine condition. It is open on Sundays throughout the year, with free entrance but donations welcome. (*Evening Telegraph*)

The romance of the golden age of steam had sadly come to an end by the 1960s along with the demise of many rural stations as much of Britain's rail network was dismantled by the Beeching axe. At one time the Kettering locomotive shed was the base for 20 passenger and mixed traffic locos, employing up to 200 drivers, fitters, firemen and cleaners. One of the last steam locomotives is pictured here at Kettering station in 1959, the same year the much-mourned Kettering to Cambridge line closed. For 93 years four trains a day used this once-popular eastern route, making no less than 14 stops on their way to the Fens. The Kettering to Manton line, opened back in 1880, lasted until 1966, losing stations at Gretton and Corby in the process. Two years later Rothwell and Desborough joined the long list of redundant stations, which locally included Cranford, Geddington, Harringworth, Glendon and Rushton, and Isham and Burton Latimer. (*Ken Fairey*)

A reminder of how radiant the dear old Kettering Grammar School building in Gold Street looked at Christmas 1957. Its diabolical demolition by Kettering Council one Sunday morning in November 1964, with no forewarning or proper public consultation, was – in the eyes of many residents – the worst single act of civic vandalism the town had ever witnessed. This elegant and atmospheric stone building, also pictured in daylight in the front end papers of this book, was erected in 1856 and used as a school until the move in 1913 to larger premises in Bowling Green Road (now the council offices), fittingly pictured in the rear end papers of this book. Ironically the council were the last occupants of the building, which in its final years was used as the borough surveyor's offices. A fuller history appears in *Old Kettering and Its Defenders*, Tony Ireson's authoritative account of the piecemeal destruction of Gold Street in the 1960s and 1970s. (*Kettering Leader and Guardian*)

Another evocative festive photograph, taken at the Gold Street traffic lights in the week before Christmas 1967. Lit up like a Christmas tree is Montagu House, the former headquarters of Kettering Industrial Co-operative Society (see page 109 for daytime view). The *Kettering Leader* of Friday, 22 December (the paper had dropped the "*Guardian*" from its title by then) reported that the Christmas lights were much better than the "pearl necklace" effect of the previous year, which caused much comment. The paper declared: "This year the lights are arranged similarly but the varying colours make them much more attractive. It seems to be a great improvement and the star-shaped lights at various junctions enhance the effect." The *Leader* added that the extra colour gives plenty of reminders of the season and ended with the observation: "Ex-Oxford Street lanterns have been popular in other towns but they are very large and apt to look like remnants from London's shopping centre. They are also apt to become battered in rough weather, so becoming more of an eyesore than a pleasure." So there! (*Kettering Leader*)

Silver Street.

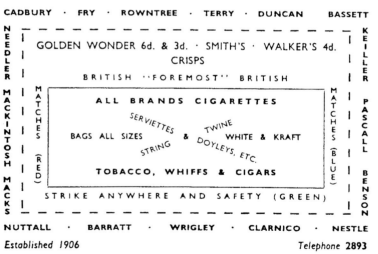

Silver Street

Cattle Market

Kettering's old cattle market in London Road (now a car park) buzzed with activity for 85 years before moving to new £200,000 purpose-built premises in Northfield Avenue in May 1965. Before 1880 markets were held regularly on the Manor House Field, but when it moved to larger grounds in London Road, hundreds of farmers came flocking into town, bringing their wives and families with them. A year after it opened the Local Board (later Urban Council) bought the land from George Lewis Watson of Rockingham Castle for £3,300, and with it the market rights granted by King Henry III in 1227. The acre-and-a-half site had previously been used as a bowling green by Benjamin Mitten and part was taken up as pastureland. In 1895 the market was extended with the purchase of land from the Duke of Buccleuch. In those days it catered annually for 2,000 cattle, 4,000 sheep and 4,000 pigs, and farmers and their families came to town by horse and trap, with livery facilities provided by the George and Royal Hotels. When the farmer had finished his business and his wife her shopping, it was the custom to return to the hotel where a meal was provided. (*Kettering Leader*)

In the early part of the century the familiar "hobo type" drovers herded their beasts into the market from all quarters. They were rarely big herds but big enough to scare shoppers or mothers with young children, when one or two strayed, and at night the drovers encamped with their stock in outlying fields. In latter years, large motorised transporters replaced the drovers, and buyers usually represented large wholesale firms. Since the day it opened, Berry Bros and Bagshaws, the Kettering auctioneers, figured prominently in market affairs (see picture) and it had been known for 800 cattle and 5,500 sheep to be packed into the market at the same time. During both world wars it built itself up as a national market, with beasts dispersed throughout the country, and later to the Continent. (*Kettering Leader*)

This historic photograph, with the municipal offices providing the backdrop, was taken on the last day of the London Road cattle market on Friday, 21 May 1965. At that time the market's annual throughput was about 22,000 cattle, 50,000 sheep and 14,000 pigs, but in some ways the market itself had hardly changed. The last alterations in London Road were 40 years earlier when a covered cattle ring and weighbridges were installed. I recall, as a young boy at junior school, spending Saturday mornings in a "secret" den a friend and I had made beneath the wooden seats of the cattle ring, until one day an attendant discovered our mode of entry and chased us off! Some 20 years later, after the *Evening Telegraph* moved to new headquarters next to the new cattle market, you had to wind your car windows up on Fridays as the fresh farmyard air drifted over. I have two more memories of the new cattle market. In September 1972, as lead singer with local rock band Blind Drunk (!), I performed at a folk-rock festival held in one of the cattle rings (John Martyn topped the bill) and during the journalists' strike of 1977, the agricultural workers' union let us use its cattle market office as our headquarters. It was the end of an era when the market closed in March 1992 after more than a century of operation. (*Kettering Leader*)

High Street

Newland Street

Market Place

Gold Street

This wonderful bird's-eye view of Gold Street was taken on 15 February 1973 from a hydraulic platform hired by A. J. Attwood of Kettering to do some repair work on the roof of Toller United Reformed Church (just out of shot. bottom right). The platform was needed to replace a piece of lead which had fallen off, and to do a complete survey, after which Jim Harker of Gotch, Saunders and Surridge declared it in surprisingly good order (apparently the last inspection had been in 1926). The platform was worth £12,000 and was often hired by BBC Television to film football highlights for *Match of the Day*. As well as the intrepid *ET* photographer who took this picture, Toller minister the Rev William McGuigan also took the opportunity to view his church from 60ft up!
(*Evening Telegraph*)

Post Office Buildings
(1887–1975)

Page 183. One of the last press pictures of the soon-to-be demolished Post Office block and arcade, taken in June 1974. Following the failure to save these historic buildings at a long-running and often heated public inquiry, the go-ahead had been given for Kettering Council to proceed with Phase 2 of the controversial town centre redevelopment scheme. First to be reduced to rubble in March that year had been Beech House in Tanners Lane (see page 84), followed by nearby Gordon House, dating back to 1800. Right to the death Kettering Civic Society battled on, but by early 1975 demolition began on these shops on either side of the arcade, the determined Francis Watts hanging on to the bitter end (see page 107) and the familiar terracotta facade finally being taken down by hand, brick by brick, to be replaced by the Newborough Centre. (*Evening Telegraph*)

Despite protests by Kettering Civic Society, this Victorian factory and pub in Northall Street were knocked down in February 1998. They were being replaced in 1999 by a £3.5 million retail development and car park, and the 25,000 sq ft site, now known as Tanner's Gate, includes a new pet store and video rental shop. The factory, a well-known local landmark, dated from 1876 and was one of the first designed by John Alfred Gotch. It began as Stockburn's corset factory, but in 1910 the premises were taken over by Geary's leather works, which moved down to the bottom on Lower Street in 1920 and closed down in 1989. For much of this century the Northall Street factory belonged to leather firm G. Stock and Son, was taken over by rag merchants Plaistere and Hanger and ended its days as Kettering Textiles, which moved to larger premises in Wellingborough. The origins of the Robin Hood pub next door were shrouded in mystery. During the early 1970s landlord Ted Reed found several old pictures of the tavern, including a painting of when it had a thatched roof, but had no idea when they were taken. Then owners, Watney Mann, could not say when the pub first opened, but official documents for the premises went back at least to 1803 and dates as far back as 1733 were mentioned in the deeds. (*Kettering Leader and, inset, Frank Corvesor*)

Chesham House

Chesham House in Lower Street, pictured here in March 1971 and in October 1998, was the ancestral home of the Gotch family. This Georgian mansion, opposite the Three Cocks pub, was built in 1762 by Thomas Gotch (1748-1806), who formed the town's first shoe and leather business in 1778. The name Chesham came from the second home of the Kettering Gotches in Buckinghamshire, where relatives were agents for the Duke of Buccleuch. Thomas, whose firm eventually employed 500 people, played a leading role in forming the Baptist Missionary Society. Indeed, the great missionary William Carey (1761-1834), in his cobbling days, would walk to Chesham House from Moulton, carrying his bag of finished boots. The Gotch family became prominent in town life for more than 150 years. Chesham House, one of only five Grade II listed buildings in Kettering, survived proposals to demolish it to make way for a car showroom in 1962 and health centre in 1971. Successive owners let it deteriorate and by the mid-1970s it became the victim of vandals and decay, with smashed windows and lead stolen from its roof. Finally the decrepit building was bought in 1976 by local builder Tony Attwood and given a facelift in 1978. It is now used as social services offices.
(*Evening Telegraph and, inset, Tony Smith*)

9. The Modern Era

A 20-year dream by town planners was realised when Kettering's controversial £3.5m Newborough Centre was officially opened by Mayor Cecil Brown on 11 December 1978. A shopping complex was first mooted in 1958 and Phase I, involving the demolition of Bakehouse Hill and building of new shops in Gold Street and Lower Street, was completed in October 1969. Phase II, funded by the council itself rather than a property developer, consisted of an indoor shopping mall and 400-space multi-storey car park. The first four stores were W. H. Smith, Sainsburys, Gayhomes and Symonds the jewellers, joined 10 days later by another nine (the Mayor had already opened Boots in September 1978). Proposals for Phase III, announced in 1982, involved almost two more acres of land, requiring the demolition of shops on the west side of Newland Street and the terrace of shops at the top of Northall Street. The Newborough Centre was sold for £8.5m to the Lazard Property Unit Trust, which spent a further £10m on the new improvements and extensions which formed Phase III. While work was being carried out, the old Richard Leys area became an unofficial car park and Sainsburys moved out of the centre to the old electricity board site in Rockingham Road. The refurbished, revamped and renamed centre (Newlands), boasting 24 new shops, officially opened on 27 November 1989. With its bright interior design, two glass lifts and marble floors, it was likened to a Las Vegas casino by Kettering Civic Society. Today Newlands is served by bus bays in Newland Street and has a wide variety of stores, selling anything from clothes, shoes, sportswear and jewellery to records, greetings cards, stationery, electrical and household goods. (*Tony Smith*)

The first of a new breed of so-called "superpubs" in Kettering was the Earl of Dalkeith, opened in December 1996 by the fast-expanding Wetherspoon chain. The group spent £1 million converting the empty building in Dalkeith Place, last occupied by furnishers F. A. Watts. The two-storey premises are open all day, offering a wide choice of real ales and food. Before planning permission was granted, there were objections from other town centre publicans who feared its competitive prices (beer from 99p a pint) would take away their trade. But the arrival of these "new kids on the block" has forced other pubs to spend small fortunes on long-overdue refurbishments in the battle for customers. Recent revamps and facelifts have included the Peacock in Lower Street (£300,000), the Swan in Montagu Street (£200,000), Watercress Harry's in Market Street (£250,000) and The Avenue in Russell Street (£350,000). The Good Companions in Hallwood Road re-opened as Goodys, the Queen in Queen Street became The Hog's Head, and even the George Hotel established a new theme bar called Georgies. The Earl of Dalkeith, incidentally, features murals of local buildings by Ron Mears and 60 framed photographs of old Kettering, all of which appeared in my first book, *Kettering Revisited.* (*Tony Smith*)

The opening of the Earl of Dalkeith sparked an explosion of interest in the Horsemarket area of town, with O'Malleys, an Irish theme pub, springing up on the opposite side of the road, and the Xtra pub, owned by Mansfield Brewery, opening in the former Liberal Club building next door. O'Malleys, pictured here, was opened in October 1997 after a £150,000 revamp by entrepreneur Brian Ward. He had previously converted the former Cross Keys Café into Mississippi's Restaurant (downstairs) and Huckleberry's Restaurant (upstairs) but closed down both after failing to obtain a drinks licence for the latter. Under landlord Alan Murdock and his wife Lucy, the bar soon established a reputation for live Celtic music. In February 1998 it was one of four finalists in the UK Music Pub of the Year contest and Lucy went on to take first place in The Licensee magazine's Bar Person of the Year in April. In September that same year the pub was granted a special hours licence allowing the upstairs function room to open until midnight from Monday to Saturday. (*Tony Smith*)

Most of Kettering's transformation during the 1990s followed the opening of the A14, the "road to prosperity" linking the industrial Midlands to the East Coast ports and Europe. The final section of the so-called M1-A1 Link, first proposed in a government White Paper in 1970, was opened on 15 July 1994 by Transport Secretary John MacGregor, after years of consultation and controversy, including a 143-day public inquiry and a series of High Court appeals by the Save Naseby Battlefield protesters. It took 24 years to plan, five years to build, employed 2,400 workers and cost £210 million – just under £5 million a mile. It boasts 33 junctions and 70 bridges over 45 miles, took up 300 hectares of land, dissected dozens of public paths and rights of way, and split 107 farms in half. It sparked off huge economic development in Kettering, now within half an hour of both the A1 and M1/M6. In anticipation of the new road, developers Arlington invested £31 million in the 92-acre Kettering Venture Park, launched in June 1990. Environmentally, much traffic has been removed from Kettering town centre, but there were soon complaints of motorists using the A14 as a racetrack. In 1998 the government gave the go-ahead for a £2.5 million lighting scheme to improve safety on the five-mile stretch from Burton Latimer to Rothwell. This picture was taken from Junction 9 looking towards Thrapston. (*Tony Smith*)

After five years of planning, the £10 million Kettering Park Hotel, owned by the Shire Inns group, opened on 2 February 1993. Sited on Kettering Venture Park overlooking the A14 (see also above picture), this luxury four-star hotel boasted 88 bedrooms, a restaurant and business centre with plush conference facilities. It also offered top-class leisure facilities, including a snooker room, swimming pool, sauna, steam room and squash courts. Business was soon booming, attracting £250,000 in advance bookings. With trade increasing after the opening of the A14, a two-floor extension costing £3 million opened in October 1997, housing another 29 bedrooms, a larger dining room and business training centre. A new gymnasium and lounge area also added to the leisure club. How the other half lives! (*Tony Smith*)

The first major firm to commit to the town was the timeshare giant RCI. The world's biggest holiday ownership company, with 800,000 members in more than 100 countries, decided to switch its European headquarters from London to Kettering. Some departments, employing 150 staff, moved to Clarendon House in Station Road (the old Canada Dry building) in 1988, but the payroll extended to more than 500 when its new £10 million offices opened on Kettering Parkway in October 1991. The striking two-tone building, pictured here, is best known to passing motorists for its distinctive digital clock. RCI, now Kettering's biggest commercial employer, was founded in 1974 in Indianapolis, Indiana, where its head office remains today. It has five other US bases plus offices in Mexico, Argentina, Australia, Japan and South Africa, and in Europe it has offices in Paris, Verona, Dusseldorf, Copenhagen, Albufeira (Portugal) and Tenerife. In 1996 it was sold to American hotel giants HFS for a staggering £400 million. Soon after it opened, the company was asked to turn down its bright exterior lights after they were dubbed "Blackpool Illuminations" by Barton Seagrave residents, upset by the glare! (*Tony Smith*)

There was much expectation when a consortium opened the £13 million Kettering Leisure Village off Northampton Road on 7 July 1993 in a blaze of publicity. But the volume of visitors to the centre from other towns was miscalculated and prices were raised after the venture fell 300,000 customers short of its target of 1.2 million for the first year. Receivers were called in on 6 October 1994 and the complex, which boasted a pool, squash and badminton courts, indoor tennis courts, health suite, an all-weather running track and floodlit football pitches, was put up for sale. Kettering Council ran it from January to the end of May 1995 when it was bought by Phoenix Leisure, and the council pledged £140,000 a year in return for a share of profits. The main hall, known as Kettering Arena, also doubles as a 3,000 capacity concert venue, and among the stars who have appeared there are Van Morrison, Squeeze, Ant and Dec, Peter Andre, East 17, Ocean Colour Scene, Paul Weller and the Manic Street Preachers. KLV still operates a laserdome for budding space warriors, but its initial ice skating rink proved unviable and closed. (*Tony Smith*)

The eight-screen Odeon cinema in Pegasus Court was officially opened on Thursday, 11 December 1997 by supermodel Caprice and TV presenter Dani Behr, with a special preview of the latest James Bond blockbuster *Tomorrow Never Dies*. By the Sunday night more than 7,000 moviegoers had visited the £6 million multiplex, paying more than £40,000. Work began in February 1997 on six acres next to the A14 at its junction with the A509 Wellingborough road. The site also includes the family pub/restaurant Hobson's Choice, an American-style Tex-Mex diner called Frankie and Bennie's and an Australian theme restaurant called Tucker's Smokehouse. The latter includes kangaroo steak on its menu and each table has a large gas "barbie" in the centre on which customers or a member of staff cook the main course with meat or fish chosen from a chilled counter. It also has TVs which children can tune into via headphones to watch cartoons. The Odeon has proved hugely popular, especially with youngsters, and early successes included *Spiceworld*, *Titanic* and *Saving Private Ryan*. (*Tony Smith*)

The trend for new theme pubs in Kettering has not been restricted to the town centre. With private housing estates springing up near the A14 junctions, breweries have been quick to move into the increasing market for "family" style taverns, all serving food throughout the day. First off the mark was Telford Lodge in Rothwell Road, complete with Charlie Chalk's Fun Factory for children, followed by The Park House, pictured here at Kettering Venture Park, owned by the Wolverhampton and Dudley Brewery. The £1.5 million complex features the 96-seater Milestone Restaurant on the first floor and a diners bar/lounge accommodating 200 people and creating 60 jobs. Kettering Mayor Bryn Morgan toasted the official opening on 5 June 1996 and pulled the first pint. One unique feature is a stair lift for elderly or handicapped diners. In 1997 The Park House was the brewery's best pub in the South East and in 1998 it also received a prestigious award for excellence by Les Routiers. The nearby Hobson's Choice, a £2 million family pub owned by pub operator Tom Cobleigh, opened on 28 November 1997, and The Trading Post, a £1.6m American frontier theme bar and restaurant owned by Mansfield Brewery, opened in July 1998 in Lake Avenue, serving the new estate near Kettering Leisure Village. (*Tony Smith*)

The gradual "Americanisation" of the former Pytchley Road area began in September 1995 when Burger King moved into Carina Road on the site opposite Tesco's superstore. The 80-seater restaurant, which created 30 jobs, was also the first in Kettering to operate a drive-through service for motorists who don't have time to sit down to eat! Then, in March 1998, it was joined on the corner of the roundabout by Fatty Arbuckle's, a diner named after Hollywood comedy star Roscon "Fatty" Arbuckle, who starred in many silent films with Charlie Chaplin and Buster Keaton. The fast-growing chain designs its restaurants on the theme of early Hollywood movies and has built 40 around the country since 1983. (*Tony Smith*)

It is only fitting, I suppose, that I should end this book with a picture of my workplace, the new *Evening Telegraph* offices at Ise Park off Rothwell Road. In my career I have now worked in all three head offices of the *ET* since it was founded in 1897 (the others being in Dryland Street and Northfield Avenue, of course). Although the 80 staff moved in at the end of June 1998, the £1.4 million complex – nestling between Telford Lodge and Kettering Crematorium – was not officially opened until the Duke of Gloucester unveiled a plaque on Tuesday, 20 October that year. At the same time the paper's new owners, Johnston Press, invested £225,000 in a new editorial computer system, said to be the most up-to-date technology in Europe. The advertising staff are downstairs and we journalists are on the first floor. Yours truly has a window seat at the rear of the building with a pleasant view overlooking the crematorium gardens – well, you can just see them through the trees. I like to think my late parents, who both departed there, are still keeping a friendly eye on me. (*Tony Smith*)

Picture Index

KETTERING URBAN DISTRICT COUNCIL.

SMALLPOX.

IMPORTANT NOTICE.

Persons who consider they are suffering from **any illness,** and are not being attended by their own Doctor, either as Private Patients or Club Patients, or under the National Health Insurance Acts, or have no Family Doctor, are requested to arrange for the **Illness to be reported** to the Sanitary Department of the Council, **High Street, Kettering, immediately,** when the case will be investigated free of expense.

By order,

JOHN BOND,

Clerk to the Council.

Council Offices, Kettering.
May, 1925.

LEADER PRESS, KETTERING. [16401]